The Psilocybin Chef
COOKBOOK

Virginia Haze and Dr. K. Mandrake, PhD

GREEN CANDY PRESS

The Psilocybin Chef Cookbook
By Virginia Haze and Dr. K. Mandrake, PhD

Published by Green Candy Press
Toronto, Canada

Copyright © 2020 Virginia Haze and Dr. K. Mandrake PhD
Photography © 2020 The very excellent Virginia Haze

ISBN: 978-1-937866-41-9

Printed in China by 1010 Printing International Ltd.

Sometimes Massively Distributed by P.G.W.

Contents

Chapter 3

Chapter 4

Chapter 5

Thanks

When we sat down to write our first book, *The Psilocybin Mushroom Bible,* we had no idea how many people were out there eager to read it. Having learned our shroom-growing craft from Paul Stamets, from the Internet and by stealing lab techniques from university and making them our own, we simply wanted to write the book we wished we'd had when we started growing so many years before, hoping that other new cultivators could avoid making the mistakes we'd made at the start. Three years later, more people have read that book than we ever could have imagined, and its success has taken us to new and exciting places. We regularly have conversations with readers, and we learn from them as often as they learn from us. This is what we love about the community; everyone is keen to educate themselves and to become better growers, consumers and people. We're so proud that our book has found its way into so many hands, and we're utterly grateful for those who've offered us support, information, gentle criticism and encouragement. We probably wouldn't have written this second book if it weren't for your requests! For this reason, we'd like to dedicate this book to you.

As ever, we remain inspired by the authors who've come before us: O. T. Oss and O. N. Oeric, better known as Dennis and Terence McKenna, who wrote *Psilocybin: Magic Mushroom Grower's Guide* back in the '70s, before either of us were even born. Little did they know what their book would create: a global revolution in home mushroom cultivation. Kerry Ogame and L. G. Nicholas also inspired us massively with the *Psilocybin Mushroom Handbook*, as did the many and varied contributors to the Shroomery, to related threads on Reddit and to the Internet at large. Roger Rabbit, too, must receive some thanks for his brilliant video *Let's Grow Mushrooms,* which is pretty much where it all began for us.

Huge thanks also must go to Green Candy Press, for turning our writings into two beautiful, high-quality books, as well as all their mentorship along the way. Here's to freedom of information.

Disclaimer

In many countries across the world, the cultivation, manufacture, possession, use and supply of psilocybin are still bewilderingly illegal. These countries include the U.S., where psilocin and psilocybin are Schedule 1 drugs (though the sale of spores is legal in most states), the U.K., where "fungi containing psilocybin" are Class A drugs, and Canada, where despite the sale of spore kits and grow kits being legal, psilocybin is illegal to possess, obtain or produce without a prescription or license.[1] [2] [3]

Schedule 1 drugs in the U.S. are those that are purported to have the following traits:

- The drug or other substance has a high potential for abuse.
- The drug or other substance has no currently accepted medical use in treatment in the United States.
- There is a lack of accepted safety for use of the drug or other substance under medical supervision.[4]

Obviously we disagree with this, due to the massive amounts of evidence to the contrary, but the law is the law.

---

[1] http://www.deadiversion.usdoj.gov/schedules/orangebook/c_cs_alpha.pdf

[2] https://www.gov.uk/penalties-drug-possession-dealing

[3] http://laws-lois.justice.gc.ca/eng/acts/c-38.8/page-26.html#docCont

[4] https://en.wikipedia.org/wiki/Controlled_Substances_Act#Schedule_I_drugs

For these reasons, we recommend that all cultivation be done in Spain, where it's decriminalized for personal use, and where they serve a damn good local beer on a hot afternoon—with a copy of our first book, *The Psilocybin Mushroom Bible,* to help you along.

The authors of this book intend for the recipes within to present a more interesting or more delicious way to consume your shrooms; these recipes do not represent the quickest way to feel the effects of shrooms, nor are they necessarily the most efficient way to consume your mushrooms. Some of the methods in this book may degrade the potency of the shrooms a little, so you might have to take slightly more to gain the same effects compared to eating dried or fresh shrooms. Some, on the other hand, are said to make the effects of the shrooms hit you faster, though these claims are always contentious as testing is so rare. The Ethanol Extraction method (page 28) and the Shroom Caps method (page 44) are the best ways to produce a consistent, reliable dose that stores well for long periods of time and has the added benefit of being almost completely tasteless. If you're only interested in long-term storage, absolutely nothing beats cracker-dry shrooms stored with desiccant in an airtight container. The rest of the recipes in the book result in food or drink that should be consumed while freshly made with a moderate dosage. We've created this book to give you delicious ways to feel the effects of psilocybin—and, we hope, to have a little fun. Please consume this book as intended.

Why Write a Shrooms Cookbook?

As dedicated psychonauts who are now unfortunately past the halcyon days of our misspent youths, we have, between us, taken mushrooms many, many times. We've had them in every possible form, and in many locations—from hostels in Peru to 5-star hotels in Paris and at many an outdoor festival with similarly spaced-out people. We've taken them recreationally and with a specific intent; to help with anxiety, to de-stress, to help us connect with loved ones we felt distant from. Throughout, one thing has remained constant: Virginia Haze absolutely *hates* the taste of shrooms.

While she struggled through her teens and twenties gagging down over-chewed fungi and gulping down mushroom tea then chasing it with something, anything with a more overpowering flavor, when she reached her thirties she decided she couldn't take it anymore. No longer would she put herself through it: she needed better methods.

Thankfully, she had Dr. Mandrake on hand.

As well as being avid mushroom cultivators, researchers and consumers, we are both gastronomic obsessives, the type who have eight different kinds of olive oil in our kitchens and who'll spend years fermenting beans with koji to make our own miso, just because we can (and because we like making a mess). Each time we tripped together, we decided to come up with a new method or recipe that was nothing short of delicious just so Ms. Haze could consume her shrooms without retching all the way through. The recipes started off simple, with basic smoothies and teas and tinctures and us having a meal together while we were experimenting, then we took the next obvious step—putting the shrooms *into* the meals. Soon we were sitting down to three-course shroom-laden dinners, each course lightly dosed so at the end of the meal we could slip on some Kula Shaker and go on a mental journey with full stomachs and happy hearts. The recipes you have in your hands are the result of that experimentation, and of our strongly held belief that if you're going to consume something, you might as well make it taste damn good.

This book starts with eight basic extractions, some of which are good for long-term storage of psilocybin and some that should be consumed immediately. From there, we go on to recipes that utilize these extractions, or into which dried or fresh shrooms can be directly placed. In the Sweets Section we'll show you how to make the types of mushroom edibles you'd get in a cannabis dispensary if you were lucky enough to live in Colorado or Canada or one of those forward-thinking places. These treats can be stored and consumed over a short time (check each recipe for how long). For the rest of the recipes, consider that the results should be consumed immediately after making, and that they are the best way to make your shrooms into a beautifully delicious meal rather than the best way to get super high. If you want to get the strongest trip as quickly as possible, stick to the Lemon Tek (if you can handle the taste) or, go the old-school way and just munch a handful of fresh or dried shrooms. Just don't expect Ms. Haze to be there with you.

For the rest of you, who like food as much as you like tripping, we hope this book goes down a treat.

The science
In magic mushrooms, the main compounds that induce the psychedelic experience are psilocybin and psilocin. Psilocin is the compound doing most of the work altering your mind in a magic mushroom trip. Psilocybin

is what is known as a *prodrug* to psilocin, in that it is not active on its own, but is broken down within the body (dephosphorylated, to be precise) to psychoactive psilocin. This dephosphorylation also occurs in acidic conditions, which is why proponents of the Lemon Tek (page 79) believe that this results in a quicker onset of the high. The theory goes that psilocybin is pre-converted to psilocin by the lemon juice itself, so you don't have to wait for your body to do this for you. It should also be noted that unlike psilocybin, psilocin is a lot less stable and won't keep its magic for as long. This is to say that you shouldn't leave your Lemon Tek sitting out for too long, as it will likely just revert back to plain old lemon juice (but with extra gross bits!). Despite this, properly dried shrooms will keep for a year or two if stored under the right conditions, with minimal loss of potency.

These two wonderful compounds belong to a group known as *substituted tryptamines*, more commonly referred to simply as *tryptamines*. They all share a similar chemical structure, and most are psychoactive—meaning that they change brain function and affect perception, mood, cognition and behavior as well as consciousness itself. Psilocybin and psilocin (as well as LSD, mescaline and DMT) are chemically similar to another substance found naturally in great quantities in the human brain: the neurotransmitter serotonin. It is this similarity that is thought to be responsible for psilocin's effect on the brain, with the general scientific consensus being that it binds to the same receptors as serotonin (5-HT2A). Our most current theory of how psilocin affects the brain is that it reduces the brain's ability both to filter incoming sensory information and to regulate connections between the different brain areas. With this ability hindered, sensory information comes in at more of a torrent than a trickle, and areas of the brain that don't frequently "talk" to each other start sliding into each other's DMs. These factors are thought to explain common experiences on magic mushrooms, such as increased interest in your surroundings and the blurring of boundaries between the different senses, otherwise known as synesthesia. So don't worry if our Shroom and Squash Burgers (page 90) taste like purple, or you can hear the delicious flavors of our Spicy

Shroom Hot Chocolate (page 77); everything is going to plan.

As previously mentioned, we have personally experimented with taking shrooms for self-betterment, from microdosing to stimulate our creative impulses to small doses of shrooms to help with anxiety, stress and to facilitate empathy in difficult situations. There have been a number of small studies along these lines, but prohibition has prevented much real research into the therapeutic or personal growth potentialities of psilocybin. Common sense tells us that what can work for one person might be totally wrong for another, but as yet we have little in the way of peer-reviewed and well-funded research to back this up, or to truly explore the ways in which psilocybin *could* be used for the betterment of society.

Historically psilocybin and other classical psychedelics have been shown to have potential benefits in treating conditions like OCD, depression and substance dependency, as well as helping those suffering from terminal illnesses. In addition there is a small interest in the psychedelic research community in what Bob Jesse, founder of the Council on Spiritual Practices and one of those instrumental in forming the psilocybin research team at Johns Hopkins University, calls "the betterment of well people"—capturing an idea that you shouldn't need a mental illness or be face-to-face with your own mortality to benefit from the psychedelic experience. Obviously, we cannot recommend self-experimentation to our readership *en masse*, and we firmly discourage using any sort of mood-altering substance (including alcohol) as a method of self-medication, but if you think that you can safely and sanely use psilocybin to help you towards becoming a person more capable of dealing with life's complications, then these recipes may help you along the way, as they are easy to dose with, can be brought into any daily routine and taste good too.

We've included information on microdosing at the back of this book, as there's currently research being done into how it (and psychedelics more generally) can be used to improve people's lives—and we've both had positive personal experiences with it, as have many others we know. One thing worth mentioning is that microdosing studies (of magic mushrooms, LSD, DMT, etc.) currently rely on surveys and reports submitted by people engaging with the practice on their own terms and at their own risk. Due to the illegality of these substances, this is currently the only viable way to collect data on the subject, as funding is scarce and the law makes the paperwork alone enough to turn many institutions away (not to mention the undeserved stigma). Despite this, there are a number of research groups comprised of individuals prepared to go through the hassle and potentially risk their reputations in order to gain a more empirical view of psychedelics and how they can be used as a treatment for those in need. We believe that it's one thing to stop people getting high for fun, but for governments to prevent credible research into potential treatments for people with mental health issues is frankly immoral. The only way that society as a whole is going to relax its moral panic around psychedelics is with well-designed studies showing their true benefits in relation to their unhysterically assessed risks. So if you're interested in getting high (if not, you shouldn't be looking at this book!), but also want to turn the tide of

prejudice against psychedelics, then consider getting involved in some research. A bit of Googling should help you find some reputable studies currently being conducted near you (or even online), but the guys over at the Multidisciplinary Association for Psychedelic Studies (MAPS) maintain an active list of studies requiring participants on their website: (https://maps.org/participate/participate-in-research).

Remember that if something becomes a crutch for you, and you begin to think that you need it to accomplish things or face the day (even if it's a cup of coffee before you think you can get out of bed), then you might need to reassess your relationship with it and how it fits into your life. Consume smartly, kids, and be the best person you can be.

The shrooms that we're working with

Mushrooms come in all kinds of wonderful shapes and sizes; whether it's the grotesque bleeding tooth fungus (*Hydnellum peckii*), the delicious morel (*Morchella spp.*), the phallic stinkhorn (*Phallus impudicus*—

literally latin for immodest penis), the beautiful amethyst deceiver (*Laccaria amethystina*) or the many bioluminescent (glow-in-the-dark) species, there's plenty to fall in love with in the world of fungi. One species of honey fungus (*Armillaria ostoyae*) including its mycelium (the fungal equivalent of a root system) is speculated to be one of the largest living organisms in the world, covering 2,200 acres. The aptly named tinder fungus (*Fomes fomentarius*) can be used to start fires and has been found on the 5000-year-old mummified corpse of Ötzi the Iceman, Europe's oldest naturally preserved mummy. Another species (*Ophiocordyceps unilateralis*) is a tropical ant parasite that takes control of its host's brain, causing it to climb up above the forest floor and anchor itself to a leaf with its jaws, where the mycelium feeds off and eventually kills its host, bursting a single mushroom out of the ant's head to release its spores into the air. With this last example, we can empathize with the ants—sometimes we feel like mushrooms have take control of our brains and made us write about them to infect others with a similar strain of fungi-fever!

But before we end up writing another book about all our favorite mushrooms, let's focus in on what we're working with in this book— magic mushrooms of the *Psilocybe* genus. Unlike more delicious species, this group of mushrooms are not famed for their culinary value (if you're looking for a great guide to wild-foraged, delicious mushrooms, then we'd recommend the books of Roger Phillips, as well as the help of an experienced forager). What they are famed for is pushing the boundaries of your mind a little and letting you see the world, and yourself, in a whole new light. Although we're the first to admit that sometimes shrooms aren't the most pleasant tasting, with this book we're trying to provide the spoonful of sugar to make the medicine go down. Whether you prefer liberty caps (*Psilocybe semilanceata*), wavy caps (*Psilocybe cyanescens*) azures (*Psilocybe azurescens*), truffles (*Psilocybe tampanensis, Psilocybe mexicana,* etc.), or the quintessential cube (*Psilocybe cubensis*), the recipes in this book will work with all of them. Do keep in mind, however, that we've calculated our doses in this cookbook based on *P. cubensis*, so if you go swapping out

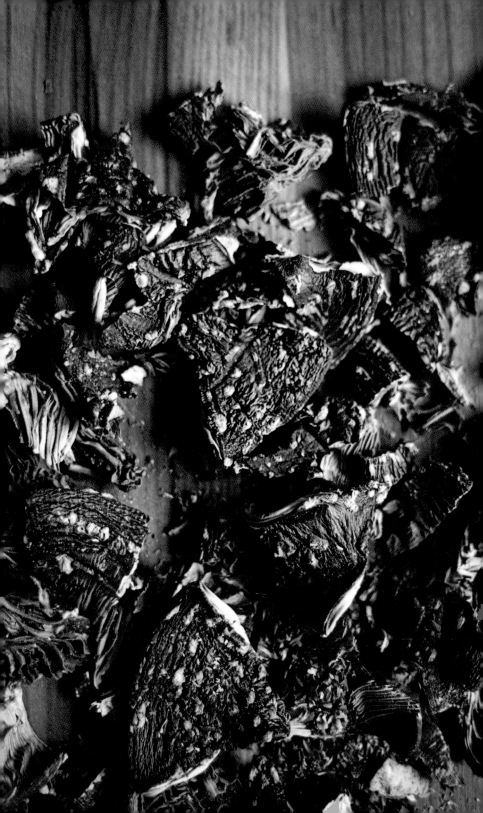

species be aware that potency can vary considerably (for example, *P. azurescens* are approximately twice as potent as *P. cubensis*).

A final word of warning on fly agaric (*Amanita muscaria*). Though some may refer to this species as a magic mushroom, it's not psychoactive in the same way as the *Psilocybe* species. Fly agaric doesn't contain psilocybin or psilocin; rather, it contains muscimol, which is the main psychoactive compound, as well as the prodrug ibotenic acid which is neurotoxic[5]. This mushroom has a fascinating cultural history of use in parts of Eastern Europe, Siberia and what is now modern-day Scandinavia, and its active compounds are equally as interesting from a pharmacological perspective, however we don't recommend it in any of these recipes. Being more toxic, and with far more unpredictable effects, if this is a mushroom that interests you proceed with caution and do your own research before consuming. And just in case someone tries to sell you *Amanita muscaria* under the guise of it being "magic mushrooms," we've included a picture of dried samples from our own enthobotanical stash on the facing page so you know what to look out for.

Does heat degrade psilocybin?

Ten or more years ago nothing could start an argument on a message board quicker than posing the question above. Today, however, besides the fact that fewer people remember what a message board is (god, we feel old), people have experimented and know a little better. Despite this, some people will still try to argue that heat degrades psilocybin hugely, throwing out intimidating scientific terms like thermal decomposition, oxidation, and the Arrhenius equation. For us, it's not that people who say heat degrades psilocybin are wrong, it's that the question is poorly stated. How much heat? How long are you heating it? How are we measuring degradation? If it was up to the good Dr. Mandrake, he'd write a research grant to approve a study, grow some shrooms and take them to the lab for detailed chemical analysis across a range of temperatures. Sadly, that sort of funding dried up a long time ago, so

---

[5] While a similar prodrug/drug relationship occurs between psilocybin and psilocin, as described on pages 6–7, it's important to note that the compounds present in the *Psilocybe* species have a far lower toxicity compared to *Amanita muscaria*.

we've had to resort to subjective self-experimentation, of which this book is a product.

   None of the recipes in this book will noticeably affect the potency of freshly grown, or even well-preserved, magic mushrooms. And if anyone tries to argue with you, hand them a hot cup of Psilo-Chai-bin (page 70) and maybe a slice of freshly baked Mushroom Banana Bread (page 119), and ask them to think over their position a little.* Or maybe after a few hours.

   For those of you who don't want to take the risk, we've included many recipes that include little to no heating at all, so you can dose and rest easy in the knowledge that you're getting the most potent punch of psilocybin possible. As for us, we'll be tucking into our Shroom and Broccoli Handpies (page 84) and having a grand ol' time regardless.

*DO NOT spike people against their best-informed consent. That's never cool.

How to dry fresh shrooms

Most of the recipes in this book will work with both dried and fresh shrooms, unless otherwise stated. We're working on the assumption that most of you will be getting your shrooms in dried form, as that's how they're typically sold (see How to Dose Your Shrooms in the next section for how to spot good vs. bad dried shrooms). However, if you find yourself in the enviable position of having a few too many fresh mushrooms and don't want them to lose their magic, you can dry them and store them for a rainy day. As natural tinkerers we've played around with lots of methods, from building weird contraptions that use fans to blast-dry the shrooms to investing in food dehydrators to really dial in the process. You can go to the same levels of nerd as us if you want, but by far the simplest method is as follows:

Place your fresh mushrooms in a single layer on something that will allow air to circulate (we found that sushi mats are great for this).

Leave them for a few days in a warm dry place, such as an airing cupboard, until they almost snap when you bend them. To finish them to optimum dryness (aka "cracker dry"), throw them in an airtight jar with a sachet of desiccant (the kind you get in new shoes or from photography supply stores) and store somewhere cool and dark.

Throw them in an airtight jar with a sachet of desiccant (the kind you get in new shoes or from photography supply stores) and store somewhere cool and dark.

Prepared this way, your shrooms will easily stay active for a year or two, or even three—though you might notice a drop in potency if you really push it!

How to Dose Your Shrooms

We're assuming that you, our dear and trusted reader, will have picked up this book having had at the very least some small experience with taking magic mushrooms before— such that you know your own tolerance and understand the basics of taking mind-altering substances and how you react to them. If you haven't taken shrooms before, the doses we are working with in this book are a good place to start, and we'd recommend consuming enough to constitute a dose (that might be a smoothie, or a few gummies, or a bowl of pasta) and waiting sixty to ninety minutes. This is how long it can take for your trip to really start, and then you can expect to feel the effects for between four and six hours, with a peak a couple of hours in. Environment and company are essential to having a good trip. Make sure you're in a safe, comfortable, relaxing place with people that you trust and enjoy; and if it's your first time, try to ensure that you're with a good friend who has taken shrooms before. The "right" dose of shrooms for any one person might be completely different to the "right" dose for another person, and because this is so subjective the only way to find out what's perfect for you is through trial and error. Still, this is beset with complications, as you might find that a dose of one gram is perfect for you on a day when you've slept well and eaten tons and have drunk lots of water, but if you're tired and you skipped breakfast and you only had a salad for lunch and you've got a slight cold that same single gram might get you much higher than you want to be. For this reason we always recommend dosing low and dosing again if you need to.

If you've read our first book, and have grown your own shrooms, you'll likely be a lot more comfortable with finding the ideal dose for you. Still, we aren't assuming you've got extensive notes on years of personal self-experimentation, so we've written this book with a varied readership in mind. To that end, we've created these recipes with low doses, as we want each one to get you on your way to being high, or give you a light buzz. As we've said before, you should always dose low, because you can take more (in this case, you can eat another slice of pie, pop another lolly or pour yourself another spiked coffee) but you cannot take less. Once it's inside you, that's where it's staying. Dose low and if you need more, you can top up with something easier on your stomach like a dosed drink (maybe the Mango Mushroom Lassi, page 75) or a candy (perhaps a Maple Shroompop, page 139); that's been our motto throughout this writing process.

However, personal tolerance varies. A six-foot-six bodybuilder might need a higher dose than a five-foot-four swimmer to get the same effect. It's up to you to dose up if you want to, but do bear in mind that getting too high is never fun. Another option is to create a full meal from these recipes that will leave you adequately trippy. If you stay with the low-dose recipes, you can pick a main, dessert and a drink from this book, building a whole menu to help you reach your desired level of high. This also allows you to stop when you know you've reached your ideal state—you can always pop a gummy snake later if you need a top-up.

All the following recipes are working to a dose of 0.5 grams dry or 5 grams wet shrooms. This is because magic mushrooms lose 90% of their weight when they are dried, but next to none of their potency. This is a fairly low dose but we find that it is the most user-friendly. The more experienced amongst you might be used to taking doses of 3.5 to 5 dry grams or more. In that case, you probably know what you're doing, so we'll trust you to dose yourself accordingly. Please bear in mind though that some of

This is product from a shake bag; old, musty, awful.

these recipes contain alcohol, which will change the way your body reacts, and also that no one is going to be impressed by you eating an entire pan of brownies and being totally out of your gourd. If you want to, that's fine, but dosing low is a responsible way to use psilocybin; don't dose high just because you think you've got something to prove.

It's worth noting here that unless you're growing your own mushrooms (and if you want to, but don't know where to start, we recommend grabbing our first book, *The Psilocybin Mushroom Bible*), it can be difficult to source high-quality shrooms to consume, let alone cook with. In the interest of ensuring that you're using well-dried and preserved shrooms for these recipes (and hopefully to make sure you don't get scammed by buying bad stuff), here's a little primer on different qualities of mushrooms.

Shake bags:

A term borrowed from the cannabis industry, a *shake bag* is basically leftovers from the growing/drying process. These bags have few fully formed mushrooms, and although smaller, unformed mushrooms are reportedly more potent, their presence is usually offset by the inclusion of non-active trash from the growing process, like bits of soil, vermiculite, perlite and/or kernels of grain. Bad suppliers will sell bags of shake at the same price per gram as primo bags, moderate suppliers will sell them at a reduced price and great suppliers won't sell them at all. Adding a little shake to primo bags can help balance out the weight, so some bags might have a little shake in. We'd say this is generally okay, but eyeball your shake-to-primo ratio and make a judgment as to whether there's a little sprinkle to get that perfect weight or if your supplier is bulking out their bags with waste.

Old bags:

Much like shake bags, the quality of *old bags* are going to vary wildly. An old bag that's been sat at the back of a cupboard may have lost considerable potency depending on how long it's been forgotten about. How do you tell old bags from primo bags? The bags themselves are usually more scuffed up, the mushrooms inside may smell unpleasant (strong damp basement smell = bad; slight damp forest floor smell = good) and they may have lost color and might be powdery. Whilst some old bags still pack a punch if preserved correctly, ask yourself the question: why does your supplier have such old product? A great supplier shouldn't have any old bags as their shrooms are in such high demand, whereas we'd question the quality of a supplier who peddles old shrooms.

This is an old bag, and will probably smell bad too.

Primo bags:

The holy grail of the shroom connoisseur, *primo bags* are the ones you want with you on your journey through the unknown realms of psyche-delic space. No shake, no old musty smell; just beautifully dried speci-mens that you'd expect to see in a natural history museum. Bonus points if your supplier has packed them in an airtight baggie with a sachet of desiccant, as this will keep out any moisture and ensure a high-potency

Primo product! Well-dried, full shrooms; you're doing well with this guy.

product for months (even years if stored right). Suppliers with primo bags care about their shrooms and clearly want you to have the best time with them, so next time you see them, give them a Gummy Shroom Snek (page 143) or a Shroomergy Ball (page 123) and tell them to keep being awesome!

A final note: There is endless debate around how, if at all, heating affects the potency of psilocybin, and while the answer is far from clear one way or the other, we have erred on the side of caution and offered many recipes that don't require heating at all. In the recipes where heating is required, we've tried to stick to a cook time of ten minutes if possible, though some have a much longer heating time. We have still felt the effects with these recipes, but if you're worried about not getting the strongest possible effects, you can always stick to the non-cook recipes. If you do get a little cavalier, or if you find that that Shroomberry Cheesecake (page 113) is just SO damn good that you've eaten three slices before you know what's happening (we've all been there), don't worry—if you get a little too high, it's not the end of the world, and we have a few tricks up our sleeves to help you feel a little less overwhelmed and plant your feet back in the real world.

What to do if you get too high

Who amongst us hasn't got a little too happy with the infused snacks, or chewed a second handful of dried shrooms, or drunk a little too much of the tea when we were young and inexperienced? There's no shame in having gone a little bit overboard with your dosing—and the good news is that there aren't any major catastrophes that can happen from consuming a little too much psilocybin; you would have to consume around seventeen kilos of fresh shrooms to do yourself any damage. The very few cases of harm caused from consuming psilocybin have been associated with combining other drugs, or with the existence of previous mental health issues in certain individuals. Basically: you're safe, and don't worry.

The worst thing to do if you've consumed a little too much is to panic, so if you feel you're getting too high, tell someone that you trust, and if you're alone (which we don't recommend), get them to come over. It's super useful to talk to someone with some experience in taking psychedelics, as they'll be able to confirm that nothing bad will happen to you, and just hearing that can really help to keep you calm. Make yourself comfortable and cozy, whether that's putting on your favorite comfies and watching the fish tank, cuddling with your dog or taking in the fresh outdoors and looking at the stars in your garden. Yoga breathing can really help here, or using something like a meditation app to keep your thoughts in context and help you gently experience any of the more intense sensations or visualizations as what they are, which is temporary and harmless. While we're talking about meditation, one of the most common themes of people having bad trips is trying to mentally run away from or gain control over the negative sensations they're currently feeling; however if you simply accept without judgment that these sensations are occurring, it may help you to "turn off your mind, relax and float downstream."

Drink lots of water, and eat if you want to; snack on something carby and sugary but only as much as you feel like. Remember that this feeling won't last forever, or in fact very long at all, and you're likely to be telling this story to your friends the following day and laughing about it.

Nausea

A commonly described unpleasant side effect of magic mushrooms is mild stomach churning and sometimes nausea. While this is something we've both experienced in the past, for us it's never been so distracting that we've not enjoyed the overall trip (and Ms. Haze is a champion puker). From personal experimentation and speaking to others, we've gleaned that there are two main ways to reduce your chances of this happening; eating lightly, and ginger.

It may sound contradictory to recommend eating lightly in a cookbook, but it's something we've found helps people prone to feeling queasy. Some of our friends go as far as fasting for the whole day before the trip, so if that's your preferred method some of the more heavy recipes in this book (like any of the main courses) might be ones to avoid. Others eat a light meal a little beforehand, so some of the lighter sweets recipes and drinks might be better suited if you've had a good time doing this in the past. We all have that one friend with a voracious appetite and an iron stomach, who can eat anything and rarely get sick, so if that's you then pick and chose among these recipes as you please. This isn't an eating competition though, so we'd recommend that beginners try the lighter recipes without alcohol first, then slowly expand their gastronomic and psychonautic horizons. It's also better to up the dosage relative to the food, so if you find our recommended dosages are too weak, top yourself up with something light like a tea (page 38) or a capsule (page 44), and note to make a stronger recipe next time!

A final word on the antiemetic (barf-reducing) properties of ginger. Ginger has been used in food and ancient medicine for many centuries, and today there is some evidence for its use as an antinausea treatment in those wanting to avoid pharmaceuticals. While the body of evidence is small and experiments sometimes flawed, a group of studies have shown that ginger can outperform a placebo for a range of nausea-inducing conditions such as chemotherapy and pregnancy. Anecdotally, we usually have a big flask of warm ginger tea (or a low carbonation ginger beer) on standby for when the occasional bout of nausea strikes. Whether it's the fresh fiery flavor momentarily distracting our brains while it's off the ranch of reality, or something more pharmacologically concrete, we're not so sure—but it definitely seems to help either way! Good recipes that include some ginger are Ginger Lime Chocolate Truffles (page 131), Basic Mushroom Tea (page 38), Electric Kool-Aid (page 67) or Tofu and Miso Shroom Stew (page 87).

Chapter 1

Extractions

These extraction methods are your starting point for the rest of the recipes in this book. While we've provided options wherever we can, and have tried to make the recipes compatible with dried or fresh shrooms where possible, some will require one of these extractions. These can also be used on their own. Some will create larger batches of material that you can dip into over time, while some are single-dose extractions to be consumed immediately. Each has an accompanying photo essay, just to make sure you can see exactly what you're doing. The rest of the recipes in the book don't need these photos, but these do. It's worth putting in the time and effort to get these right. Trust us!

There are many benefits to using the extraction methods that follow, but to our minds the most important is that they help you to homogenize dose between a mixed crop of mushrooms that may vary in potency. Let's say you have the remnants of three different grows; a fresh batch of your own, some that a mate gave you a month ago and some that you found in the back of your underwear drawer from two years ago. The fresh ones are likely to be a hell of a lot stronger than the ones that have been hanging out with your tighty whities, and can you ever know the potency of some that you haven't grown yourself? By extracting the psilocybin from all of these together, you'll have a stable extraction, the potency of which you'll know from first usage. Some of these methods, such as the Ethanol Extraction, allow for long-term storage in a fridge or freezer, while others, such as the capsule-making method (not technically an extraction) allow for easy consumption and storage somewhere dry and cool.

27

Ethanol Extraction

Extracting psilocybin into ethanol (high-strength alcohol) is both easy and convenient. Compared to extractions into normal alcohol, it evaporates faster and will leave you with a much smaller volume of the resulting liquid. When it comes time to trip, you'll only need a couple of drops of an Ethanol Extraction; with a well-mixed solution, dosing is consistent and accurate, and you can mix a couple of drops of your extract into any other liquid for ease of consumption. Storage as well is incredibly easy; your extraction will be kept in a light-resistant dropper bottle, meaning that it can be kept in your fridge or freezer and out of sight of everybody else. Kept in the freezer, it will remain viable for a year or two. We use this method for accurate microdosing.

The downsides of this method are that the shelf life of the extract is relatively hard to predict when kept at room temperature, and even when kept in the fridge or freezer for longer periods of time. Some might find the technique a little too time consuming for them, though we haven't found this to be the case. The main drawback to this method, however, is that—as with all liquid extractions—it can be very easy to get carried away and overdose yourself. Instead of a few drops, you do several more, and then you're higher than you ever intended to be. Maintain a low dosing technique with alcohol extractions; remember, you can always take more.

Despite the simplicity of this method, it has to be completed over a few days. This shouldn't be an issue; it's a do-and-leave sort of technique. You'll need to have purchased a dark-glass 20-millimeter dropper bottle—these are widely available online—and you'll also need a coffee filter and a clean syringe. Everclear is a commercial alcohol that comes in both 151- and 190-proof versions (75 and 95% ethanol respectively), and you can absolutely use these types for this extraction, but you can also buy bottles of high-proof ethanol online or from medical supply stores. The late Alexander Shulgin (an incredible chemist who personally synthesized over 230 psychoactive compounds) recommends an optimal percentage of 70% ethanol, which you can dilute your chosen ethanol source to with water. We've found that 75–95% ABV (151–190 proof) works fine. However, be careful with this as some spirits (usually called denatured alcohol in the U.S.) contain methanol, which is *highly* toxic and is added to allow companies to avoid paying tax on for-consumption alcohol (don't get us started on how shit this is). Do NOT use methanol, or anything other than ethanol, for this extraction. Some techniques online call for you to extract the psilocybin into methanol before evaporating all the methanol and adding ethanol. Just cut out the middleman and use ethanol; far easier, far safer.

For 0.5 grams per dose, you'll want to use 10 grams of dried mushrooms per 20 milliliters of ethanol. We've found this to be a good midpoint, but of course feel free to experiment with stronger or weaker extracts as per your needs. If this is your first alcohol extraction, however, stick to the amounts we've suggested and then find out what strength you prefer through trial and error.

After soaking the mushroom material in the alcohol, our method calls for you to leave the liquid out in the air for the ethanol to evaporate. The extent to which the alcohol evaporates doesn't matter, because you'll measure what amount of liquid you have left and add more ethanol to bring it up to 20 milliliters; this allows for correct dosing, as the psilocybin content stays the same no matter what the overall volume of the liquid. However, if you leave the ethanol out too long, you might find that you end up with a sticky film on your dish but little else, leaving you panicking that all the solution has evaporated. Don't worry; it hasn't. You can revive your sticky solution by taking 20 milliliters of ethanol and "washing" the dish with it. This will resuspend the extract and everything should be fine. We know this works thanks to the inability of one of us to follow basic instructions.

It's also possible to extract psilocybin from dried, used PF Tek cakes (the substrate on which you'll grow shrooms in the PF Tek method; you can learn about this in our first book *The Psilocybin Mushroom Bible*) using the method above. When you've harvested your PF Tek cakes, break them up into little chunks and put them in the same place as your harvested mushrooms and let them dry out in the same way. They need to be bone dry before you begin. In theory, you can then use the dried cakes in much the same way you've used the mushrooms above. In general, mycelium contains less psilocybin than shrooms themselves on a weight-for-weight basis. However, it's difficult to estimate exactly how much weaker cakes are compared to shrooms, with some recommending at least six cakes for a noticeably potent extraction. Therefore, it can be difficult to know exactly how strong this extraction from cakes will be, so if you've used a fair few, exercise caution when dosing. You may want to leave the PF Tek pieces in the alcohol a little longer than normal, to extract as much of the remaining psilocybin as possible.

If your cakes exhibit any signs of mold or other contamination, don't use them. Toss them. It's not worth the risk.

Ingredients
100 milliliters 75–95% ethanol
10 grams dried shrooms

Servings
20 (1 milliliter of Ethanol Extraction = one 0.5-gram dose)

Method

1 Assemble all your kit (electric spice grinder, scales, funnel, coffee filter, measuring flask, alcohol and dried shrooms).

2 Weigh out 10 grams of dried shrooms.

3 Add the shrooms to the spice grinder.

4 Blitz them up real good, until you have a fine powder.

5 Measure out 100 milliliters ethanol (conical flask optional).

6 Add the powdered shrooms to a clean jar.

7 Pour the ethanol over the jar of powdered shrooms.

8 Swirl or stir it all up.

9 Put the lid on the jar and leave it somewhere dark overnight.

10 The next day, give the jar a good shake and pour the slurry through a coffee filter into another container. You might find some of the slurry stays in the jar. Use a little splash of alcohol to wash this out into the filter.

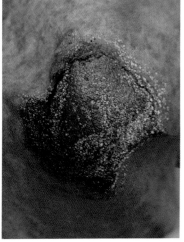

11 Patiently wait for all the liquid to drain through.

12 Gently squeeze the last few drops out. We mean gently! If you burst the filter into your extract you'll have to re-filter it.

13 Pour the extracted liquid into a clean, shallow baking dish, and let it evaporate down to 20 milliliters. The gentle breeze of an electric fan can help here, but don't be tempted to heat it! Try not to let it evaporate down to a paste as it will start to lose its potency, but if you end up with less than 20 milliliters simply top it back up with ethanol.

14 We like to store our extract in these little brown dropper bottles. The ones we found dose out a single milliliter (equivalent to 0.5 gram of dried shrooms), which we mix in a glass of fruit juice and are good to go. You'll notice the liquid in this picture might be a bit darker than your extract; that's due to this bottle being around a year old. We stored ours in the freezer, and it still did the job a year later!

Shroomshine

aka Simple Spirit Extraction

This method is very similar to the previous one, but as it uses normal-strength, readily available alcohol you may not get quite as good an extraction efficiency as you do with the ethanol recipe. Also the potency of this extract will drop off a fair bit faster so this recipe is therefore recommended for immediate use and for adding to your favorite cocktails (see our favorite cocktails in the Drinks section). Compared to the previous recipe, you'll get more of a booze effect and less of a shroom effect (though you'll feel both).

Ingredients

400 milliliters white rum, vodka or your preferred spirit

2 grams dried shrooms

Servings

4

Method

1 Assemble all your kit (electric spice grinder, scales, funnel, coffee filter, measuring flask, alcohol and dried shrooms).

2 Weigh out 2 grams of dried shrooms.

3 Measure out 400 milliliters of your favorite spirit (we won't judge you if it's not rum!).

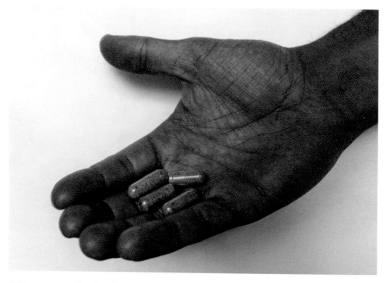

4 You can powder the shrooms in an electric spice grinder as in the other extractions, or you can also empty out four 0.5-gram capsules if you've made these already (page 44).

5 Add the powdered shrooms and alcohol to a clean jar or bottle.

6 Give it a swirl to mix everything up.

7 Leave the jar in a dark place for around 24 hours. We find it's helpful to label jars with doses and dates, especially if you have a few extractions on the go at once like we do!

8 After 24 hours, pour the boozy shrooms through a coffee filter into another container.

9 Let all the liquid filter through until you're left with the sludge in the bottom of the filter. You can toss this out.

2g
P.cubensis
in
400ml
white
rum

10 Put your Shroomshine in a labeled bottle, so you know which one will get you extra wavey at your next cocktail party. We've had success storing this for up to a week in the fridge.

Basic Mushroom Tea

The second most popular way of consuming shrooms is to make a tea, which can be done with either fresh or dried shrooms. This is a very simple method that allows for quick uptake, although it's not the most pleasant tasting. It's fairly easy to dose with this method, although there can be some slight variation between doses, and sometimes you can come up *too* quickly. To avoid this, sip the tea; don't throw it down your throat.

If you're using dried, you might want to first grind your mushrooms to a powder, which can be done using a coffee or spice grinder. You can use your normal coffee grinder (as long as you clean it thoroughly afterwards, or your morning cup is going to get a lot more interesting) but we prefer to have a dedicated grinder for shrooms, so there's no cross contamination of flavors (or psychedelic material). You can make tea with whole shrooms, in which case just finely chop them up.

There are a number of different ways to make your mushroom tea a bit more palatable. Here we've added lemon, honey and green tea, though you can use any kind of tea bag that you prefer, as long as it masks the woody taste of the shrooms. We also like to add ginger, as you'll see in the recipe below. The ginger helps to relieve any nausea while you're coming up and the honey makes the mixture a little nicer to the taste buds. Experiment and find what works best for you.

Ingredients

10 grams fresh/1 gram dried mushrooms

500 milliliters boiling water

2–3 green tea bags (we like gunpowder green, but feel free to use your own favorite tea)

juice of ½ a lemon

a thumb-sized piece of fresh ginger

1 tablespoon honey/agave (more if you like it sweeter)

Servings

2 (1 tea = 0.5-gram dose)

Method

1 Every Mad Hatter knows that you can't have a tea party without a good tea set!

2 Powder your dry shrooms as in the previous recipes, or finely chop them if they're fresh. Add this to the jug of boiling water.

3 Thinly slice the fresh ginger and add this to the jug.

4 Add the tea bags…

5 …and squeeze in the lemon juice. Don't worry about the bits as we're going to be filtering all this.

6 Give it a good stir and let the mixture steep for 15–20 minutes.

7 Pour the mixture through a coffee filter into your teacups.

8 Add honey to taste. Sip slowly with your pinky extended like the high-class bastard you are!

Paul Stamets' Ice Water Blue Juice

This extraction comes courtesy of Our Holy Father Paul Stamets, and was first described in his *Psilocybin Mushrooms & The Mycology of Consciousness* lecture at the Multidisciplinary Association for Psychedelic Studies Psychedelic Science Conference in April 2017.

This is the simplest possible extraction method, and though it may take 24–48 hours for best results, it's very much a love-it-and-leave-it method. In fact, it's so easy that there's no photo essay necessary; instead, you can gaze on the final product's beauty. You may see some ultra-blue versions of this online, but we suspect foul play and food coloring; the natural color is a hazy navy blue, and it's gorgeous. All you need is fresh shrooms and ice.

Ingredients
5 grams fresh shrooms
100 grams ice cubes

Servings
1

Method
1 Take your fresh shrooms, clean them of any detritus, and chop them as finely as you possibly can.

2 Place the chopped shrooms in a clean glass jar with the ice. Give it a good shake.

3 Put the jar into the fridge and leave it for 24 hours.

4 Strain the resulting liquid through a fine sieve and discard the mushroom bits.

5 Drink immediately or freeze the blue juice into four ice cubes for later use.

Shroom Caps

If you can't be bothered to try any of the recipes or other consumption methods in this book, then the single best thing that you can do is to invest in a cheap capsule-making kit and start making your own mushroom capsules. It's incredibly easy but has an incredible amount of benefits. You can buy these kits from any sort of online head shop or even on some larger retail sites, and if you're uncomfortable buying things online they can be fairly easily sourced in real life. All you'll need to make the dried mushrooms into powder form is a regular coffee grinder, though it's preferable here to use an old one or have one that's only used for this purpose.

One of the benefits of making capsules is that you can be sure of getting an exact dose every time (or as close as is possible), and it can be a lot easier to manage your consumption when things are in capsules as opposed to in tea or in mushroom form. Because they're in powder form, the onset should be faster, and you avoid all the grossness of the taste. If you're vegan or vegetarian, it's easy to find capsules that suit your dietary requirement at health food stores or online. Capsules are also easy to transport without worrying about people finding your shrooms. Keep them in a prescription medicine or nutritional supplement container and they'll appear to be any normal type of medication. This is definitely stealthier than carrying around baggies of dried shrooms on a night out or a wander in the forest.

The downside to putting your mushrooms into capsules is that it can look a bit sketchier, as you can't tell if pills contain just shrooms or other substances. This is especially important for psychedelics, where your starting mindset plays a huge role in the chances of your enjoying the experience. Only share with friends who you trust, and who trust you. And, in fact, you shouldn't take mushroom capsules when offered to you unless you trust the person and know them well; one powder can be easily exchanged for another and you could end up taking an unknown dose of an unknown substance, or just bunk filler, instead of the mushrooms that you wanted. Be smart, kids.

Our preferred dose when making shroom capsules is 0.5 gram in a 00 capsule. This allows you to get a moderate trip, or to double up and get a stronger experience. Using 26 grams will make 52 caps. If you make a few of these and want to store them for a while, pop a desiccant packet in the container holding the capsules to keep that pesky moisture out.

Ingredients

12 grams dried shrooms

24 00-sized capsules (get the vegan-friendly ones if you are)

optional: 1.2 grams powdered ginger root

Servings

24.

Method

1 Assemble your kit. Capsule makers and capsules can be sourced online with a quick web search.

2 Weigh out 12 grams of dried shrooms.

3 Blitz up the dried shrooms to a fine powder.

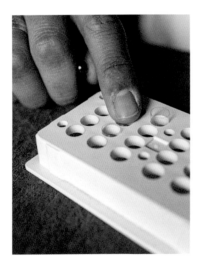

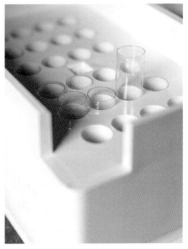

4 Follow your capsule maker instructions. This usually begins with placing your capsule shells into the two halves of the machine.

5 As one half of the capsule is slightly bigger, make sure you've got the right halves in the correct part of the machine. They should fit in snugly, without having to either force them in or have them rattling around loosely.

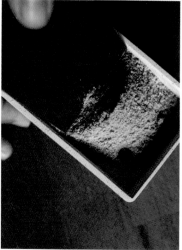

6 Gently pour the powdered shrooms into the base of the capsule maker. It sometimes helps to have this set up on a plate to catch any bits you might spill. Certainly don't do this on a rug!

7 Use the supplied card, or a credit card to spread the powder across all the holes.

8 Tamp down the powder into the holes, making sure everything is lined up correctly.

9 After you've pressed the powder down, there'll be more space in the holes to catch the extra powder.

10 Use the card to repeat the procedure until all the pills are full.

11 Firmly press the top of the capsule maker down on to the base to seal the capsules.

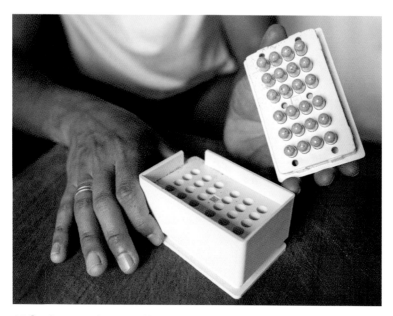

12 Gently remove the top, making sure that all the capsules lift away from the base.

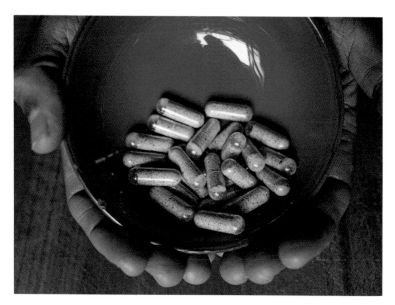

13 Use bowl to catch the capsules as you press them out of the machine. Store all your capsules in an airtight jar with a sachet of desiccant, and they'll keep their potency for at least a year!

Basic Warm Milk Extract

There's a long-held belief in some sections of the community that psilo-cybin and dairy just don't go together. This is based on the idea that lactose and/or casein do bad things to psilocybin, such that drinking milk with your shrooms can or will "kill your trip." This is based on no scientific evidence, and from personal experience we can tell you that this isn't the case.

We love this milk extract as you can do a whole bunch of things with it, as you'll see later in this book. You can also drink it straight, or if you're fancy, add some matcha powder and honey to it for a Japanese-inspired drink.

Ingredients

10 grams fresh/1 gram dried mushrooms

1 cup milk (dairy free for lacto-intolerant/vegans)

Servings

2 (½ cup = 0.5-gram dose)

Method

1 This recipe is pretty simple; you'll just need your mushrooms and a cup of milk.

2 Weigh out 1 gram of dry or 10 grams of fresh shrooms.

3 Add the cup of milk to a pan and begin to heat. Stir frequently so that it doesn't burn to the bottom of the pan.

4 Once the milk is near boiling, add the powdered dry shrooms, or finely chopped wet ones.

5 Remove the pan from the heat, and allow the mixture to infuse for 15–20 minutes.

6 Pour the mixture through a clean cloth (muslin or cheesecloth are perfect, but a clean tea towel will work in a pinch).

7 Make sure you get all the little bits out of the pan for maximum magic!

8 Spice up your warm milk with flavors like chocolate or Psilo-Chai-bin, to complement the taste.

Blue Honey

We recommend making Blue Honey (or shrooney as we will call it forever more) as needed and using it all, as there is a very small but serious risk of botulism when this product is been stored for a long time. Mushrooms store perfectly well dry, so this recipe should be viewed as a step in a bigger recipe rather than as a long-term storage method. If you're going to store it (we don't recommend this) Blue Honey is probably good for about two weeks if properly refrigerated. as the bacteria responsible for botulism don't like acidic environments, a splash of apple cider vinegar in the jar will help reduce the risks of storing this product (this isn't necessary for freshly made Blue Honey which you intend to use immediately).

Although we don't recommend storing your shrooms in honey, if you come across a jar in the back of the fridge (or a friend gives you a jar) it's good to know some telltale signs to help you avoid bad batches. These are:

- Very runny consistency, closer to water than honey.
- Fizzing/hissing when the jar is opened.
- Small rising bubbles in the honey, or a foamy layer on top.
- Mold/discolored patches on the surface.
- Unpleasant smells (Parmesan cheese/vomit/poop).

If you come across any of these in your Blue Honey, throw it out immediately. We don't want to scare people, but the best advice is make fresh, use immediately and you'll have nothing to worry about! Some people will say we're being overly cautious, but we just don't want to take that risk. If you do, that's up to you.

A note: Blue Honey is traditionally so-called because it's said to turn blue if your fresh shrooms are bruised when you dry them; in turn, the honey supposedly turns blue. We think this is something of an urban myth, but we like the name—so sue us.

Ingredients

2 grams dried shrooms, ground or blended to a powder

¼ cup high-quality honey

Servings

4

Method

1 This is another simple procedure, though technically not an extract as the original shroom material stays in the honey.

2 Powder the 2 grams of shrooms with an electric spice grinder, and add to the honey.

3 Then, basically, leave it til you need to use it!

4 It will tend to separate over time so give it a good stir again just before you use it. Keeping it in the fridge will crystallize the honey and prevent the separation from occurring, which is another option.

Basic Coffee Extraction

Feel free to use whatever method you prefer (French press, V60, mocha pot, etc.), as long as you mix the mushrooms in with the coffee. We're using Aeropress because we're snobs.

Most Aeropress recipes use around 15 grams of coffee of a medium-fine grind with around a 1–2 minute brew time. For this recipe we went for a coarser grind with a cooler water temperature to allow for a longer mushroom extraction. There are plenty of coffee aficionados out there with lots of different opinions on what goes into the best cup, so feel free to experiment, bearing in mind a longer brew time will get more out of your mushrooms but might over-extract your coffee. We find a low acidity lighter roast also helps avoid this, but some people swear by a coffee so strong you can stand a spoon in it, so you do you.

Ingredients

15 grams coffee—coarser grind for longer extraction

0.5 gram dried shrooms, ground or blended to a powder

1 cup water at 185°F/85°C, or just before your kettle reaches a rolling boil.

Servings

1

Method

1 Assemble your favorite overly complex kit for making coffee. Any method where the ground coffee and shrooms can sit in water for a while will work, such as inverted Aeropress or French press. Methods such as pour-over, mocha pots and even espresso machines won't work as well here due to the minimal contact time between the water and shrooms.

2 Weigh out the 0.5 grams of powdered dried shrooms, or powder them after weighing.

3 Add the 15 grams of ground coffee to the Aeropress. If you have the ability to change your grind size, go a little coarser than usual to allow for a longer steep time.

4 Add the powdered shrooms.

5 Pour the hot water into the Aeropress.

6 Stir it all up for a nice, even extraction.

7 Put the cap on, making sure not to forget your filter!

8 Set a timer for 3 minutes. This is longer than we'd normally brew coffee for, but we have found it helps give the shrooms time to extract.

9 After 3 minutes are up, flip the Aeropress over a cup.

10 Press down slowly but firmly.

11 Serve your coffee with or without milk and sugar—however you like it!

Chapter 2

Drinks

Sometimes the quickest and easiest way to get something inside of you is to drink it, and sometimes this is the most delicious way too. In this section we'll show you a number of easy recipes for drinks that are huge improvements on the filthy-tasting tea that we've all suffered through too many times—well, apart from the Lemon Tek, which is in many ways awful tasting, but which is such a strong part of shroom-taking history that we couldn't help but include it here. If you are hardcore, go Lemon Tek (page 79). You have our blessing.

A note regarding combining alcohol with psilocybin: some people find that this simply doesn't work for them, and that the presence of the alcohol can put them in a slightly different place than where they want to be when they're tripping. This isn't the case for everyone, and we've found that a low amount of alcohol (and we do mean low) can help relax us and can in fact enhance the effects of the mushrooms; this is, according to the pure speculation of esteemed scientists, because alcohol breaks down into several metabolites including acetaldehyde, which reacts with the body to produce monoamine oxidase inhibitors (MAOI), which in turn are known to prolong and/or enhance the effects of psilocybin. As people who have turned to shrooms after a few too many drinks, we can say that although it can be fun, you should proceed with caution—especially if you're an emotional drunk. If you do fancy a stagger down this path, start light on the booze and see what works for you. We've had friends take shrooms so wasted that they have passed out and come to tripping and freaking out. Don't be that guy, and start with one or two of these cocktails while tripping.

Doors of Perception

Ingredients

1 shot vodka Shroomshine (page 34)

1 shot blue curaçao

4 shots lemon juice

crushed ice

maraschino cherry to garnish

Method

1 Fill highball glass with crushed ice.

2 Pour over vodka extract and blue curaçao.

3 Top off with lemonade/juice.

4 Add cherry.

Servings

1

Prep Time

2 minutes

Trippy Mary

Ingredients

2 shots vodka Shroomshine (page 34)

4 shots good-quality tomato juice

½ shot lemon juice

few dashes of Worcester sauce (OR soy sauce for veggie/vegan OR tamari for gluten free/veggie/vegan)

Tabasco/hot sauce to taste

salt/celery salt to taste

crushed black pepper to taste

ice cubes

mushroom powder and celery to garnish

Method

1 For mushroom salt rim (optional but awesome), mix powdered mushrooms with salt in 1:1 ratio in a shallow plate.

2 Take a wedge of lemon and run it around the glass edge. Invert glass and spin edge through mushroom powder.

3 Half fill highball glass with ice, pour over liquid ingredients.

4 Add hot sauce, salt and pepper to taste and stir well.

5 Garnish with celery stick.

Servings

1

Prep time

2 minutes

Little Fluffy Clouds

Ingredients

2 shots white rum Shroomshine (page 34)

6 shots pineapple juice

2 shots coconut cream

ice cubes

pineapple wedge and maraschino cherry
to garnish

Servings

1

Prep time

2 minutes

Method

1 Pour liquid ingredients into blender,
add crushed ice and blend until slushie
consistency is reached. Serve.

Electric Kool-Aid

Believe it or not, beets pair amazingly well with the taste of mushrooms, as do apple and ginger, and this is the sort of drink you can have at brunch without anyone batting an eyelid.

Ingredients

1 gram dried mushrooms/10 grams fresh

2 cups apple juice

2 cooked beetroots

2 thumb-sized pieces of ginger

juice of one lime

honey/agave to taste

fresh mint to garnish

Servings

2

Prep time

5 minutes

Cook time

15 minutes

Method

1 Heat apple juice in pan until just boiling.

2 Powder dry mushrooms/roughly chop freshies, thinly slice ginger and add to hot apple juice.

3 Simmer for 10 minutes, then add chopped beets and honey to taste and allow to cool.

4 Blend until smooth, then strain liquid through muslin.

5 Half fill highball with ice, then pour over liquid leaving room for a splash of soda.

6 Garnish with fresh mint leaves.

Blueberry Shroomie

If you want to make this but don't have fresh shrooms to hand, you can use Basic Warm Milk Extract (page 50) instead of the milk, or Blue Honey instead of the honey (page 52).

Ingredients

10 grams wet (fresh) shrooms

½ cup blueberries

1 banana

1½ cups almond milk (or milk of your choice)

1 tablespoon honey

Method

1 Place all ingredients in a blender, with a few ice cubes if you prefer.

2 Blend. Enjoy.

Servings

2

Prep time

2 minutes

Cook time

2 minutes

Psilo-Chai-bin

Ingredients

1 cup milk (dairy, almond or soy)

1 cup Basic Warm Milk Extract (page 50)

2 cups water

3 black tea bags

2-inch piece of fresh ginger

1 cinnamon stick

3 cloves

3 cardamom pods, crushed

3 teaspoons agave nectar/maple syrup

Servings

2

Prep time

5 minutes

Cook time

10 minutes

Method

1 Place everything into a pan over a medium heat, bring to a boil, then cook for 5 minutes.

2 Remove from the heat and let sit for 5 more minutes.

3 Drain and serve!

Salt-Sweet Lassi

Ingredients

2 cardamom pods

1 cup Basic Warm Milk Extract (page 50)

1 cup milk

2 tablespoons coconut cream

1 tablespoon honey/agave

¼ teaspoon salt

Servings

2

Prep time

5 minutes

Cook time

5 minutes + 2 hours

Method

1 Crush the cardamom pods and get the seeds out. Throw the pod away. Grind the seeds in a pestle and mortar with the salt.

2 Heat additional cup of milk and add to Basic Warm Milk Extract.

3 Add coconut cream honey/agave and the cardamom and salt mixture, then whisk well.

4 Allow to cool, then refrigerate for 2 hours before serving.

5 Sprinkle mushroom dust on top if you like!

Mango Mushroom Lassi

Ingredients

¼ teaspoon garam masala powder

1 cup warm milk extract

1 cup natural yoghurt (or dairy-free coconut yoghurt for vegans)

2 ripe mangos

Honey/agave to taste

Servings

2

Prep time

5 minutes

Cook time

5 minutes + 2 hours

Method

1 Allow warm milk extract to cool to room temperature.

2 Add chopped mango, natural yoghurt and honey/agave to taste.

3 Blend until smooth and refrigerate for 2 hours before serving.

4 Sprinkle mushroom dust on top if you like!

Spicy Shroom Hot Chocolate

Ingredients

1 small cinnamon stick

seeds of ½ a vanilla pod

¼ teaspoon dried chilli

1 cup Basic Warm Milk Extract (page 50)

1 cup milk

100 grams dark chocolate

honey/agave to taste

Servings

2

Prep time

5 minutes

Cook time

10 minutes

Method

1 Heat the cup of milk and add to Basic Warm Milk Extract. Add the cinnamon stick, vanilla seeds, chili and warm through.

2 Add chocolate and honey/agave to taste, whisk well until the chocolate has melted.

3 Strain out the spices.

4 Aztecs traditionally drank chocolate cold, unlike the Mayans who drank it hot. Drink immediately for a Mayan-style drink, or allow to cool to room temperature and/or refrigerate for 2 hours before serving for an Aztec-style drink.

Lemon Tek

The earliest reference we could find to this tek (Internet shroomspeak for technique) is a 2005 shroomery.com thread by Underhillmaster that begins, "To tell you the truth, I am not sure I should even be telling anybody this, but I feel like I have to." To this day the thread still continues to generate the odd post every few months, and currently sits at around 1,400 posts.

This is the good old-fashioned Lemon Tek. Some say it's placebo effect, others swear by it. All we know is it tastes awful but we've included here for historical purposes.

The theory behind this method is that instead of waiting for the acids and enzymes in your stomach to break down the mushrooms, you're creating an outside environment for that to happen in; namely, the acid in the lemon juice. Thus the psilocybin starts to break down into psilocin before you've ingested it, allowing your body to just grab hold of that psilocin when you swallow the liquid and send you off on that trip before you know it. It's worth noting that these claims are made by people on the Internet, and there is very little evidence that this actually occurs.

You'll need to use the juice of a lemon; make sure that the liquid completely covers your ground-up shrooms. If you choose to leave the solution for longer than 30 minutes, then there may be a more advanced breakdown of psilocybin and you'll likely get higher quicker. However, we think that 30 minutes is about right.

Use real lemon juice for this method, not the stuff out of a bottle.

Ingredients

0.5 gram dried mushrooms, blended to a powder

juice of one lemon

Servings 1

Prep time 1 minute

Cook time 30 minutes

Method

1 Add mushroom powder to lemon juice and stir. Leave to sit for 30 minutes.

2 Enjoy (as much as is possible).

Chapter 3

Main Courses

While we've stuck with tradition and named these dishes "main" meals, they certainly shouldn't be considered as the stars of this particular show; they contain the same dosage as the rest of the recipes in this book, and like all the others are intended to present a tasty way to consume your shrooms rather than the best way to get the strongest effects. If you're inviting a friend over for a night of gazing into the cosmos and want to line your stomachs while you lay down the groundwork for a tripsy eve, these recipes are perfect.

These meal-sized dishes will require a little more cooking than many of the other recipes in this book, but we've included a variety so that you can pick and choose. The easiest and quickest are either the Grilled Cheese Shroomwich (a classic, page 98) or the Shroomlette (page 95); the gastronomically inclined among you won't mind putting a little more effort into the Shroom and Squash Burger (page 90) or even the Risotto ai Funghi di Bosco (page 83). While the flavor combination in this last one might seem a little off the wall, mushrooms and blueberries are often paired together in high-end restaurants as they are a traditional flavor pairing, and this dish is based on an old Northern Italian dish called *risotto del bosco*: risotto of the woods.

Risotto ai Funghi di Bosco

Ingredients

1 onion, diced

1 cup mushrooms

2 grams dried shrooms powdered OR

20 grams fresh shrooms, finely chopped

2 tablespoons fresh thyme + a little
more for reserve

2 cups Arborio rice

1 ½ cups dry white wine

5 cups vegetable stock

1 cup shredded spinach

1 ½ cups blueberries

salt and pepper

olive oil

Servings

4

Prep time

10 minutes

Cook time

45 minutes

Method

1 In a large pan, heat the oil over a medium-high burner and then add in the onion and cook until it's translucent.

2 Add in the mushrooms and cook for another 3 minutes, stirring often.

3 Add in the fresh thyme and Arborio rice, and stir to ensure everything is coated in oil.

4 Add in the dry white wine and stir well.

5 Cook, stirring often, until most of the liquid is absorbed by the rice.

6 Add in ½ a cup of the veg stock, and cook again until most of the liquid is absorbed.

7 Keep adding in ½ a cup of the veg stock until it is all gone, and the rice is done but still has a little "bite" in it. Add the shrooms in with the final ½ cup of stock.

8 Remove the pan from the heat.

9 Stir in the salt, pepper and a little more fresh thyme, and then very gently stir in the blueberries.

10 Serve with a little garnish of fresh thyme, and if you have time, a blueberry reduction for the top; just simmer down the leftover blueberry juice when the last ½ cup of the stock is still left to go, then drizzle the thick reduction over.

11 Enjoy!

Shroom and Broccoli Handpies

Ingredients

1 pack puff pastry (make sure it's vegan if you are)

1 onion, roughly chopped

2½ cups button mushrooms, chopped

1 gram dried shrooms, powdered OR

10 grams fresh shrooms, finely chopped

1 cup broccoli, chopped

2 cloves garlic, crushed

½ teaspoon cumin

1 teaspoon garam masala

⅔ cup coconut milk

olive oil

Servings

2

Prep time

10 minutes

Cook time

70 minutes

Method

1 Preheat the oven to 350°F/175°C. In the meantime, heat a little oil in a pan and fry the onion and garlic until the onion is browning.

2 Add in the mushrooms, broccoli, garam masala and coconut milk, and stir well.

3 Cook for 10–15 minutes, until the liquid has reduced and the vegetables are tender.

4 Remove from the heat and stir in the shrooms.

5 Roll out the sheet of puff pastry and cut in half.

6 Place half the filling in the middle of each portion of pastry.

7 Wet along the edges of the pastry.

8 Fold the pastry over the filling and pinch the top crust together with the bottom crust all the way around, creating an edge on each pie. Crimp with a fork if you're fancy.

9 Cut 2 holes in the top of each pie, then cook for 20–30 minutes.

10 Serve!

Tofu and Miso Shroom Stew

Ingredients

2 cups mushrooms, sliced

1 gram dried shrooms, powdered OR 10 grams fresh shrooms, finely chopped

150 grams very firm tofu, diced

1 onion, diced

1 clove garlic, crushed

1 tablespoon miso

1 cup hot water

½ teaspoon cumin

1-inch piece of ginger, grated

1 tablespoon vegetable oil

black pepper

Servings

2

Prep time

10 minutes

Cook time

30 minutes

Method

1 Fry the tofu separately in a little oil for 10 minutes, then remove from pan and set aside.

2 Fry the onions and the garlic in the remaining oil for 5 minutes.

3 Add miso paste to the hot (but not boiling) water, stir well and add to onions and garlic.

4 Add black pepper, tofu, ginger and cumin.

5 Allow to simmer until it has reduced almost to desired consistency. The water should have evaporated.

6 Add the mushrooms and shrooms to the stew and cook for 5 more minutes.

7 Serve over rice.

Creamy Garlic Shroom Pasta

Ingredients

1 cup mixed mushrooms of choice

1 gram dried shrooms OR 10 grams fresh, powdered or finely chopped

2 cloves garlic, crushed

1 cup milk

1 tablespoon wholemeal flour (white would also be fine)

½ teaspoon herbes de provence

2 tablespoons olive oil

150 grams dried spaghetti

bunch fresh parsley

Servings

2

Prep time

5 minutes

Cook time

20 minutes

Method

1 Cook half the garlic in half the olive oil for a minute, then add sliced mushrooms and shrooms.

2 Cook for few minutes and set aside.

3 Bring a pan of salted water to the boil, add in the spaghetti and cook for 10–12 minutes until al dente.

4 Cook remaining garlic in remaining oil, add flour and herbs and stir well until combined.

5 Slowly whisk in the milk, add cooked mushrooms and a handful of parsley and cook for a few minutes.

6 Stir through cooked spaghetti and garnish with parsley; freshen with a squeeze of lemon.

Shroom and Squash Burger

Ingredients

500 grams butternut squash (peeled, seeds removed)

½ cup oats

⅔ cup wheat gluten

½ cup cooked bulgur wheat

2 grams dried shrooms, powdered OR

20 grams fresh shrooms, finely chopped

½ cup pumpkin seeds

small bunch chopped cilantro

1 tablespoon cumin powder

½ tablespoon smoked paprika

½ tablespoon cayenne pepper

½ tablespoon onion powder

½ tablespoon dried oregano

½ tablespoon dried basil

olive oil

balsamic vinegar

salt and pepper

Servings

4

Prep time

10 minutes

Cook time

90 minutes

Method

1 Preheat oven to 400°F/200°C.

2 Cut butternut squash into 1-inch cubes. Toss with a little oil and the herbs and spices.

3 Roast for 30 minutes, stirring once or twice.

4 Add the pumpkin seeds and a few dashes of balsamic vinegar, stir through, and roast for a further 15 minutes.

5 Leave the roast squash to cool for about 10 minutes, and combine the oats and wheat gluten in a large bowl. Add dried shrooms here, if using.

6 Once cool enough to handle, puree the squash mixture with a blender until smooth. You might still have a few chunks of pumpkin seed left, but that's okay. Add in fresh shrooms here, if using, and puree with the squash. Season to taste.

7 Roughly chop the cilantro, and add it to the dry ingredients along with the puree and cooked bulgur wheat.

8 Stir everything together, then get your hands in there and shape into individual burgers.

9 Fry in a pan over a low heat, flipping over so as not to burn.

Cream of Shroom Soup

Ingredients

6 cups button mushrooms, chopped

2 grams dried shrooms, powdered OR

20 grams fresh shrooms, finely chopped

2 medium onions, diced

2 cloves garlic, crushed

2 tablespoons plain flour

4 cups hot veg stock

½ cup coconut milk oil

black pepper

Servings

4

Prep time

5 minutes

Cook time

30 minutes

Method

1 Fry the onion and garlic in a little oil until soft and translucent.

2 Add in the mushrooms and shrooms, stir well and cook for 3 minutes.

3 Add the flour and stir well to coat.

4 Add the stock and bring to the boil.

5 Bring down to a simmer for 10 minutes.

6 Allow to cool, then blend.

7 Season and reheat.

8 Stir in coconut milk to taste and serve immediately.

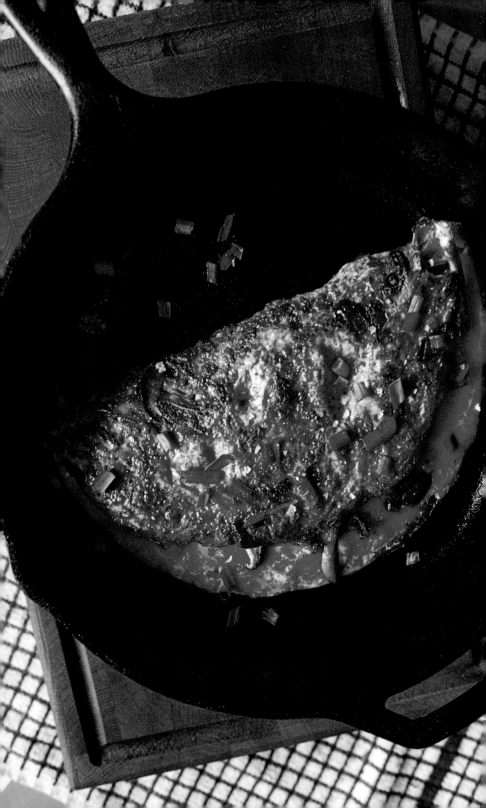

Shroomlette

Ingredients

2 eggs

25 grams butter

½ cup mixed mushrooms

0.5 gram dried shrooms, powdered OR

5 grams fresh shrooms, finely chopped

½ red pepper, sliced

3 green onions, sliced

Servings

1

Prep time

5 minutes

Cook time

10 minutes

Method

1 Beat the eggs together in a bowl.

2 Heat a heavy pan and melt the butter in it.

3 Add the red pepper, mushrooms, shrooms and half the green onion to the pan and cook for 2–3 minutes.

4 Add the beaten egg to the pan and cook on low heat for 5 minutes until the top is almost set.

5 Flip half of the omelette onto the other half as shown in the picture.

6 Top with the rest of the green onion and slide onto a plate to serve.

Shroomshuka

Ingredients

2 tablespoons olive oil

1 onion, sliced

3 garlic cloves, crushed

1 large yellow pepper, sliced

2 tablespoons harissa paste

1 tablespoon tomato paste

1½ cans diced or crushed tomatoes

1 teaspoon ground cumin

pinch of ground cinnamon

2 large handfuls fresh spinach

1 gram dried shrooms, powdered

OR 10 grams fresh shrooms, finely

chopped

sea salt

freshly ground black pepper

2 eggs

Servings

2

Prep time

5 minutes

Cook time

30–40 minutes

Method

1 Heat the oil in a frying pan and add in the onion and garlic over a medium heat.

2 When the onions are turning translucent, add in the yellow pepper and cook for 3–4 minutes.

3 Add in the harissa and tomato pastes, stir well, then add in the diced/crushed tomatoes.

4 Add in the cumin and cinnamon, stir well, then bring the heat down to a simmer.

5 Let the mixture cook for 10–15 minutes, until it's just starting to reduce.

6 Add the spinach and the shrooms into the frying pan and season to taste. Cook for another minute or two.

7 When the spinach is starting to soften, make two gaps in the mixture and crack the eggs into the sauce. Cover.

8 Cook until the eggs are just set.

9 Top with a little sea salt and black pepper, then remove from the heat. Transfer the pan to a heatproof serving plate on your table and serve straight from the pan, with lots of crusty bread to mop up the sauce.

10 Enjoy!

Grilled Cheese Shroomwich

Ingredients

4 slices good quality sourdough

200 grams of your favorite cheese; we used Camembert and Shropshire blue (because we're British) but you could use whatever you want.

2 tablespoons red onion marmalade

1 gram of ground shrooms

olive oil

good quality butter

Servings

2

Prep time

5 minutes

Cook time

15 minutes

Method

1 Butter the bread.

2 Top two of the slices of bread with the cheese.

3 Top each cheese layer with half of the ground shrooms.

4 Spread the other two slices of bread with the marmalade.

5 Press together one cheese slice and one marmalade slice to make a sandwich and butter the outsides of the bread.

6 Repeat with the other slices to make a second sandwich.

7 Heat a griddle pan and fry each sandwich on each side for 3–4 minutes

8 Slice and serve with a side salad, pickles and a cold beer.

Pulled Jackfruit and Mushroom Tacos

Ingredients

1 tablespoon vegetable oil

½ red onion, finely chopped + ½ red onion, sliced

1 teaspoon ground cinnamon

2 teaspoons smoked paprika

2 tablespoons BBQ sauce

½ can chopped tomatoes

20-ounce can young jackfruit in brine, drained

½ cup water

1 gram of ground shrooms

4 hard-shell tacos

1 avocado, sliced

fresh cilantro to serve

Method

1 Heat the oil in a frying pan and add the finely chopped onion.

2 Fry for 10 minutes until soft.

3 Add the cinnamon and paprika to the onions. Cook for 2 minutes.

4 Add BBQ sauce, tomatoes, jackfruit and the water. Simmer gently for 45 minutes.

5 Shred the jackfruit with a fork and stir in the dried shrooms.

6 Split between the taco shells, then top with sliced avocado, the sliced red onion and fresh cilantro.

Servings

2

Prep time

5 minutes

Cook time

70 minutes

Chapter 4

Desserts

Ah, the classics. The first thing that many of us did when trying to shroom-spike our meals was to throw a handful of badly dried mushrooms into a pan of brownies, or into a milkshake, hoping that the sugar and the cocoa would cover up that woody flavor—and it did! Consider these recipes not a replacement for that method, but an enhancement of it.

While we've tried to stick to our own rule of not cooking shrooms for more than ten minutes, just in case some of you still want to play it safe regarding degradation of psilocybin from the introduction of longer heating, some recipes just aren't possible without a longer exposure to heat—and while you *could* just eat spoonfuls of brownies mixture if you really wanted to, we feel quite strongly that it's better if you bake it.

As ever, we've included some recipes that miss out the heating of the mushroom content altogether, just for you. Our biggest warning here though is not to get carried away with the unbelievable taste of the Shroomberry Cheesecake (page 113) and eat the whole pie, because although you certainly won't regret it in terms of flavor, your stomachache and the resultant intensely massive high might not be what you were aiming for. If you do want to go nuts with the cheesecake, just leave out the shrooms. It's just as good without.

Shroom Jell-O

Ingredients

2 grams powdered dried shrooms

80 grams Jell-O powder

400 milliliters hot water (or as per packet instructions*)

Optional: dried, shredded coconut

*We used Ahmed brand raspberry Jell-O, as it's vegan and so are we. In reality you can use any brand of Jell-O you prefer and follow the instructions on the packet.

Servings

4

Prep time

5 minutes

Cook time

2 hours

Method

1 Add powdered shrooms to Jell-O mix in a bowl.

2 Add hot water and stir. Allow to set to room temperature then refrigerate for at least two hours before serving. Serve sprinkled with dried, shredded coconut, whipped cream, or whatever else your decadent self is in the mood for!

Bonus points: to make the Amanita muscaria style Jell-O you see in the pictures, find a wide deep plate that you're certain is going to hold all your liquid Jell-O mix (a pasta plate is ideal). Once your Jell-O is set, take a cake stand of similar diameter to your Jell-O plate (if you can't match up the sizes, slightly smaller is better than slightly bigger) and invert it over your Jell-O plate. Flip the plate and cake stand back upright; if your Jell-O is clinging to the plate use a silicone spatula to encourage it to loosen its grip (be careful with your cake stand positioning here, as we've nearly dropped the whole Jell-O on the floor countless times!). If your cake stand is slightly too big and/or you have overhanging Jell-O, use a knife to gently cut away the excess. Sprinkle with dried, shredded coconut for that final touch of toadstool!

Chocoshroom Nutty Pie

Ingredients

For the crust:

1 cup finely ground almonds/almond meal

1 cup oat flour

4 grams dried shrooms, ground or blended to a powder

4 tablespoons agave nectar (or Blue Honey (page 52), if you want each slice to give a stronger dose)

4 tablespoons melted coconut oil

a pinch of salt

For the filling:

3 large bananas

1 cup 100% natural peanut butter

¼ cup coconut oil

2 tablespoons cocoa/raw cacao powder

1 tablespoon agave (or maple syrup)

a pinch of salt

Servings

8

Prep time

10 minutes

Cook time

30 minutes

Method

1 In a food processor, blend together the almond meal, oat flour, sweetener, shrooms, coconut oil and salt until it's a fine mixture.

2 Grease a pie dish and press the crust into it tightly. Place the crust in the fridge.

3 Place the bananas, peanut butter, coconut oil, sweetener and salt into the food processor and blend for 5 minutes, or until the mixture is light and airy.

4 When the mixture is ready, remove ⅓ of it from the food processor and set aside.

5 Add in the cocoa powder/cacao to what's left in the food processor and blend again until mixed.

6 Remove the crust from the fridge and spread the chocolate filling evenly inside.

7 Place in the freezer for 15 minutes, then remove from the freezer and spread the non-chocolate mixture on top.

8 Freeze until you're ready to eat. Defrost in fridge for 12 hours before eating.

Cookies and Shroom Ice Cream

Ingredients

1 cup whole milk OR 1 cup Basic Warm Milk Extract (page 50)

2 cups heavy cream

¾ cup caster sugar

seeds of 1 vanilla pod

1 cup crumbled chocolate sandwich cookies

2 grams dried shrooms, ground or blended to a powder. If you're using Basic Warm Milk Extract as above, only use 1 gram dried shrooms.

Servings

4

Prep time

40 minutes

Cook time

2–3 hours

Method

1 Gently heat the milk, cream, sugar and vanilla seeds together in a pan, whisking to combine.

2 Remove from the heat and allow to cool fully.

3 Stir in the shrooms.

4 Transfer the mixture into your ice-cream maker and freeze according to manufacturer's instructions, gently pouring the crumbled biscuits in as the mixture churns.

5 When the ice-cream maker is done, transfer the mixture to the freezer for 2–3 hours, then enjoy.

Crepes with Shroomberry Compote

Ingredients

Compote:

1 cup frozen blueberries

2 tablespoons water

¼ cup granulated sugar

juice of 1 lemon

1 gram dried shrooms, ground or blended to a powder

Crepes:

1 tablespoon butter + reserve

½ cup flour

1 large egg

¾ cup milk

pinch of salt

Servings

2

Prep time

20 minutes

Cook time

20 minutes

Method

1 Sift the flour into a mixing bowl with a pinch of salt.

2 Make a well in the center, then crack the egg into it.

3 Whisk together, then add the milk in a drizzle while whisking, until you get a fully combined batter.

4 Set aside for 15 minutes.

5 In a small saucepan, combine the blueberries, water and sugar.

6 Bring to the boil, then bring down to a simmer for 10 minutes, stirring often.

7 Remove from the heat, adding in the lemon juice and the shrooms.

8 Melt some of the reserved butter in a frying pan and wipe it with kitchen roll to ensure it's covered.

9 When the pan is hot, pour a ladleful of batter into the pan, tilting the pan quickly so the batter forms a circle.

10 Cook for a minute until it comes away from the pan, then lift with a spatula and flip.

11 Cook for another minute, then slip it onto a plate.

12 Repeat with the rest of the batter, folding the crepes into neat triangles.

13 Top each plate with half the compote and serve.

Shroomberry Cheesecake

Ingredients

2 cups Graham Cracker crumbs

6 grams dried shrooms

½ cup butter, melted

1 cup blueberries

3 cups cream cheese

½ cup heavy cream, cold

juice of 1 lemon

1 teaspoon vanilla extract

Servings

12

Prep time

30 minutes

Cook time

1 hour

Method

1 Place the Graham Crackers and shrooms into a food processor and blend until it's all crumbs.

2 Add the melted butter and blend until the mixture comes together.

3 Press evenly into the bottom of a 20-centimeter/8-inch springform pan.

4 In a bowl, whisk the cream cheese until it's soft, adding in the lemon juice and vanilla extract.

5 In a smaller bowl, whip the heavy cream until it holds soft peaks, then gently fold into the cream cheese mixture.

6 Set ⅓ of the mixture aside.

7 Take the rest and pour it into the pan, smoothing with a spatula, then place in the fridge.

8 In a separate bowl roughly crush the blueberries until most are popped.

9 Take the remaining mixture and mix the blueberries into it, leaving some more intact than the others.

10 Top the cheesecake with this blueberry-flecked mixture, smooth down the top, then place in the freezer for an hour.

11 Remove from the pan (it should come off easily) and keep in the fridge until ready to consume.

Mocha Mushroom Brownies

Ingredients

2 cups all-purpose flour

1 cup sugar

½ cup cocoa

1 teaspoon salt

1 teaspoon baking powder

1 teaspoon vanilla essence

1 cup very strong instant coffee (3 tablespoons coffee to 1 cup water)

1 cup vegetable oil

1 cup mixed chopped nuts; we used walnuts, pistachios and pecans.

½ cup dark chocolate, roughly chopped

4 grams dried shrooms

a squeeze of lemon juice

sea salt flakes for top

Servings

8

Prep time

20 minutes

Cook time

20 minutes

Method

1 Preheat your oven to 350°F/180°C. In a bowl, stir together the flour, sugar, cocoa, salt, baking powder and orange rind.

2 In a smaller bowl, stir together the coffee, oil, vanilla essence and orange juice.

3 Stir the wet ingredients into the dry, then stir in the almonds, walnuts, shrooms and dark chocolate chunks.

4 When combined, pour the mixture into an 8 x 8-inch greased baking tray.

5 Top with sea salt flakes.

6 Bake for 20 minutes, or until a toothpick comes out clean.

7 Allow to cool, slice and enjoy!

8 Lie down in a darkened room to recover.

Shroom-Spiked Milkshake

Ingredients

2 scoops ice cream of your choosing (to double-dose this recipe, use Cookies and Shroom Ice Cream on page 108)

1 cup Basic Warm Milk Extract (page 50)

1 tablespoon honey

Servings

2

Prep time

2 minutes

Cook time

2 minutes

Method

1 Place all ingredients in a blender, with a few ice cubes if you prefer.

2 Blend.

3 Enjoy.

Mushroom Banana Bread

Ingredients

2 cups plain flour

1 cup brown sugar

3 very ripe bananas, mashed

1 teaspoon vanilla essence

1 teaspoon baking soda

1 teaspoon baking powder

pinch of salt

²/₃ cup coconut oil

pinch of ground cinnamon

pinch of ground cardamom

5 grams dried shrooms, ground or blended to a powder

Servings

10

Prep time

15 minutes

Cook time

50 minutes

Method

1 Preheat the oven to 350°F/180°C.

2 Sift together the flour and sugar, then stir in the baking powder, cinnamon, cardamom, baking soda, ground shrooms and salt.

3 In a smaller bowl, stir together the coconut oil, vanilla essence and mashed banana.

4 Add the wet ingredients to the dry and stir until just combined.

5 Pour the mixture into the loaf pan and drop it onto the countertop a few times to even it out and get rid of bubbles.

6 Bake for 50 minutes, or until a toothpick comes out clean. Do NOT bring it out of the oven until a skewer right in the center comes out clean.

7 Turn out onto a cooling rack and leave it until it's properly cooled.

8 Slice and serve.

Blue Honey Flapjacks

Ingredients

½ cup butter

½ cup brown sugar

½ cup Blue Honey (double batch page 52)

2½ cup oats

Servings

8 big ol' flapjacks

Prep time

10 minutes

Cook time

20 minutes

Method

1 Preheat oven to 350°F/180°C.

2 Gently heat the butter, Blue Honey and sugar together in a pan until the butter has melted.

3 Add the oats and stir well.

4 Press into a greased 20 x 30-centimeter/8 x 12-inch baking pan

5 Bake for 15–20 minutes, until browning on top.

6 Cut into squares while the baked mixture is cooling in the pan.

7 Turn out when cool and serve.

Shroomergy Balls

Ingredients

6 grams dried shrooms, ground or
blended to a powder

½ cup ground almonds

½ cup cocoa powder

¼ cup grated coconut + reserve for
coating

4 tablespoons almond butter

1 teaspoon vanilla essence

Method

1 Place all ingredients into a food
processor and blend until the mixture
comes together into a ball.

2 Roll into 12 equal-sized balls.

3 Roll in the reserved coconut.

4 Keep Shroomergy Balls in the fridge
or eat immediately.

Servings

12

Prep time

15 minutes

Chapter 5

Sweets

S omewhere along your mushroom-taking journey you've probably learned the time-honored trick of slathering your shrooms
in dark chocolate to (semi-successfully) hide the taste. This is
one of the simplest ways to make shrooms more palatable, and it
works. But we're afraid that it just wasn't enough for us, so in this section you can find a range of sweet treats that are so delicious you'll forget that they contain shrooms at all.

Our favorite here is the Ginger Lime Chocolate Truffles (page 131)
which first appeared in our debut book. The ginger in this recipe helps to
stave off any nausea, and we've taken these to parties, festivals and
camping trips dozens of times and got nothing but crazy positive feed-
back about them—one of our friends even had them confiscated on the
way into a club, as they didn't believe anyone would be so endearingly in-
nocent as to bring homemade chocolates to an all-night warehouse party
(they were right, but he was let in anyway!). They can't fail, in our opinion.

The gummy and lollipops recipes here are very much inspired by those
you'll find in cannabis dispensaries all over North America. We find that these
offer a really good way to microdose, especially on the go; if you're a fan of
eating breakfast then microdosing before you get to college, no one will bat
an eyelid at a student with a lollipop on the bus, and by the time you sit down
to start your work or your research you'll be getting that nice feeling of well-
being and creative stimulation that we all know and love. Some of these
recipes are more stable than others and therefore can be stored for longer,
but essentially work on the idea that these, like the other recipes in the book,
should be consumed as quickly as possible after they've been made.

While the simpler recipes in this section can be made with things

you'll likely already have in your kitchen, some of the others will probably require the purchase (or borrowing) of a couple of items you don't
already have. Thankfully, these are both cheap and widely available, and
can be used over and over again, not only for shroom edibles. For this
reason, we think they're a worthwhile investment (and we hate filling
our kitchens with unnecessary gadgets; Virginia won't even have a
toaster as she says it's a waste of time).

To make the lollipop and Shroom Shatter (page 147) recipes here,
you'll need a candy thermometer; there's no way around this. We've
actually got a laser thermometer that was fairly cheap, works well and
makes us feel like futuristic super-villains, but any old candy thermometer will do. For these recipes you'll also need to master the process of
bringing your mixture to the "hard crack" stage, where you'll bring the
sugar solution to 300°F/150°C then quickly pull it from the heat, at
which point you'll add in the psilocybin-containing material so it doesn't
get aggressively heated (just in case).

To make a real chocolate bar with the Shroom and Sea Salt Dark
Chocolate recipe (page 128), you'll need a chocolate bar mold. For the
lollipops and the gummies (and perhaps the Shroom Shatter), you'll
also need molds. We prefer silicone molds, as they're easy to use and
even easier to clean after the messy business of candy making. They
also come in all sorts of shapes and sizes, so you could even get
mushroom-shaped molds if you so wanted (we didn't). These usually
come in variety packs or individually, so you can get as few or as many
as you want, and they're not too pricey. Well worth it, we think, for the
joy of presenting your friends with a bowl full of shroom-laced gummy
bears at a party one night. They'll love you for it!

One important note: It's absolutely essential that, if there are kids in
your house, even just on occasion, you keep dosed candies well se-
cured and out of the reach of anyone who is underage. These may look
like candies, but they are not intended for the consumption of children.
If you make edibles that look like candies, it is your responsibility that
they're not mistaken for normal confectionary by kids—or by anyone
that doesn't know they're dosed. Be a responsible psychonaut!

Shroom and Sea Salt Dark Chocolate

Ingredients

100 grams dark chocolate

2.5 grams dried shrooms, ground to a powder

pinch of sea salt flakes

¼ teaspoon coconut oil

Servings

5

Prep time

5 minutes + 30 minutes to set

Method

1 Set a glass bowl over a pan of water and bring the water to a simmer.

2 Place the chocolate into the bowl and gently stir until melted.

3 Remove from the heat and add in the coconut oil, shroom powder and salt.

4 Stir well and pour into your chocolate-bar mold.

5 Set in the fridge for 30 minutes, remove, pop out of the mold and enjoy!

6 Store in the fridge for up to a week.

Ginger Lime Chocolate Truffles

These are always a hit. The ginger in this recipe acts as an antiemetic—that is, it works to counteract the nausea that many people feel when consuming shrooms—and the lime juice begins the breakdown of psilocybin to psilocin before it enters your body, making the come-up a little faster. This makes the trip from these seem very intense. We've had doses as low as 0.75 grams before and after fifteen minutes we were trying to lock ourselves into someone's spare room that was (for some reason) filled with tiny musical instruments. Dose low; you can always take more.

Ingredients

50 grams dark chocolate

65 grams crystalized ginger

6 grams dried shrooms, ground or blended to a powder

zest of ½ a lime

juice of ¼ lime

Servings

12 (1 chocolate = 0.5-gram dose)

Prep time

10 minutes + 30 minutes to set

Method

1 Slowly melt the chocolate in a bain-marie or double boiler.

2 Blitz the crystallized ginger almost to a paste (your new shroom-powdering electric spice grinder works a treat for this).

3 Add in the lime zest, lime juice and blend again.

4 Tip into a bowl, add the powdered mushrooms and stir to combine. It will look like goblin poo at this point.

5 With damp hands, form the mixture together and roll it out into a long thin log.

6 Cut into 12 equal-size pieces, then roll each one into a ball.

7 Either roll each ball in the melted chocolate or, if using truffle molds, cover the bottom of the mold with melted chocolate, add the ball of mixture then top with more chocolate to cover completely.

8 Place in the fridge to set for 30 minutes.

9 Consume immediately, or within a few days for the best effects.

Shroom and Superfood Chocolate Bark

Ingredients

100-gram bar of your favorite chocolate

a handful of your favorite superfood toppings: chopped nuts, goji berries, dried raspberries, coconut shavings, etc.

2.5 grams dried shrooms, ground or blended to a powder

salt

Servings

5

Prep time

15 minutes

Method

1 Set a glass bowl over a pan of water and bring the water to a simmer.

2 Place the chocolate into a bowl and gently stir until melted.

3 Cover a baking tray in Saran Wrap or use a silicone baking mat.

4 Spread the melted chocolate onto it and quickly top with your toppings, shrooms and a little salt.

5 Leave to set then break into 5 pieces.

6 Enjoy.

Lemon Shroompops

Ingredients

1 cup white sugar

½ cup light corn syrup

¼ cup water

1½ teaspoons lemon extract

yellow food coloring

10 milliliters of Ethanol Extraction (page 28)

Servings

10 lollipops, depending on your molds.

1 lollipop = one 0.5-gram dose

Prep time

5 minutes

Cook time

25 minutes

Method

1 Combine the sugar, corn syrup and water in a medium saucepan over a medium-high heat.

2 Stir until the sugar is totally dissolved and bring to the boil, then stop stirring.

3 Place your candy thermometer (or point your laser) in the pan and when it reaches 300°F/150°C, pull the pan off the heat straightaway.

4 Wait until the temperature cools to 250°F/120°C, then add in the extract, a couple of drops of food coloring and the Ethanol Extraction. Stir to combine. Note: Alcohol is flammable, so make sure the pan is near NO open flames at this point.

5 Lay one lollipop stick into each mold hole, then pour the mixture into your lollipop molds, being sure to cover the stick completely.

6 Cool at room temperature for an hour then pop candies out of the molds.

7 Store in an airtight container away from children for up to a month.

Sour Orange Shroompops

Ingredients

1 cup white sugar

½ cup light corn syrup

¼ cup water

1½ teaspoons Seville orange extract

orange food coloring

10 milliliters of Ethanol Extraction (page 28)

¼ cup caster sugar (icing or regular)

1½ teaspoons citric acid

Servings

10 lollipops depending on your molds.

1 lollipop = one 0.5-gram dose

Prep time

5 minutes

Cook time

25 minutes

Method

1 Combine the sugar, corn syrup and water in a medium saucepan over a medium-high heat.

2 Stir until the sugar is totally dissolved and bring to a boil, then stop stirring.

3 Place your candy thermometer (or point your laser) in the pan and when it reaches 300°F/150°C, pull the pan off the heatstraight away.

4 Wait until the temperature cools to 250°F/120°C, then add in the extract, a couple of drops of food coloring and the Ethanol Extraction. Stir to combine. Note: Alcohol is flammable, so make sure the pan is near NO open flames at this point.

5 Lay one lollipop stick into each mold hole, then pour the mixture into your lollipop molds, being sure to cover the stick completely.

6 Cool at room temperature for an hour then pop candies out of the molds.

7 Mix the citric acid and sugar together in a bowl, then half dip each lollipop into the mixture, or fully if you're just that kind of renegade.

8 Store in an airtight container away from children for up to a month.

Maple Shroompops

Ingredients

2 cups pure maple syrup

10 milliliters of Ethanol Extraction (page 28)

Servings 10 lollipops depending on your molds

Prep time

5 minutes

Cook time

25 minutes

Method

1 Pour the maple syrup into in a medium saucepan over a medium-high heat.

2 Bring to a boil, then stop stirring.

3 Place your candy thermometer (or point your laser) in the pan and when it reaches 300°F/150°C, pull the pan off the heat straightaway.

4 Wait until the temperature cools to 250°F/120°C, then add in the Ethanol Extraction. Stir to combine.

Note: Alcohol is flammable, so make sure the pan is near NO open flames at this point.

5 Lay one lollipop stick into each mold hole, then pour the mixture into your lollipop molds, being sure to cover the stick completely.

6 Cool at room temperature for an hour then pop candies out of the molds.

7 Store in an airtight container away from children for up to a month.

Apple Juice Psilocybin Gummy Bears

Ingredients

¾ cup pure apple juice (with or without pulp, your choice!)

½ teaspoon lemon juice

2 teaspoons agar-agar (for vegan gummies) OR 2 tablespoons gelatin

1½ tablespoons honey, agave or another liquid sweetener

20 milliliters Ethanol Extraction (page 28) OR 10 grams powdered shrooms

Servings

100 mini-bears (depending on your molds).

5 bears = one 0.5-gram dose

1 bear = one 0.1-gram microdose

Prep time

5 minutes

Cook time

10–15 minutes

Method

1 Place the apple juice, sweetener and lemon juice in a medium saucepan and gently heat until warm. Do not bring to a boil.

2 Add in the agar-agar or gelatin super slowly and whisk until combined.

3 Remove from the heat and stir in the Ethanol Extraction or the powdered shrooms. Note, if using ethanol extract: Alcohol is flammable, so make sure the pan is near NO open flames at this point.

4 Carefully pour or spoon the mixture into your gummy molds, or if you have a cooking syringe, use that. It's a lot easier.

5 Refrigerate for 4 hours.

6 Store in an airtight container in the fridge, away from children. Consume within 2 weeks.

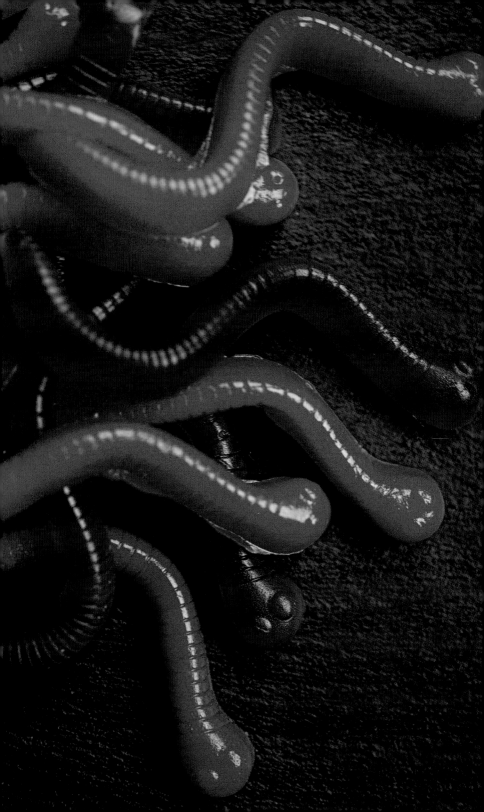

Gummy Shroom Sneks

Ingredients

¾ cups pomegranate juice

½ teaspoon lemon juice

2 teaspoons agar-agar (for vegan gummies) OR 2 tablespoons gelatin

1½ tablespoons honey, agave or another liquid sweetener

6 grams of dried shrooms, ground to a powder OR 12 milliliters of Ethanol Extraction (page 28)

Servings

12 servings (2 sneks = one 0.5-gram dose)

Prep time

5 minutes

Cook time

10–15 minutes

Method

1 Place the pomegranate juice, sweetener and lemon juice in a medium saucepan and gently heat until warm. Do not bring to a boil.

2 Add in the agar-agar or gelatin super-slowly and whisk until combined.

3 Remove from the heat and stir in the Ethanol Extraction or the powdered shrooms. Note, if using extract: Alcohol is flammable, so make sure the pan is near NO open flames at this point.

4 Carefully pour or spoon the mixture into your gummy snek molds, or if you have a cooking syringe, use that. It's a lot easier.

5 Refrigerate for 4 hours.

6 Store in an airtight container in the fridge, away from children. Consume within 2 weeks.

Note: If you want to use this recipe for microdosing, use 2.4 grams of dried ground shrooms or 4.8 milliliters of Ethanol Extraction. This will give you 1 microdose per snek.

Sour Gummy Shroom Sneks

Ingredients

¾ cups juice of your choice

½ teaspoon lemon juice

2 teaspoons agar-agar (for vegan gummies) OR 2 tablespoons gelatin

1½ tablespoons honey, agave or another liquid sweetener

6 grams of dried shrooms, ground to a powder OR 12 milliliters of Ethanol Extraction (page 28)

¼ cup caster sugar (icing or regular)

1½ teaspoons citric acid

Servings

12 servings (2 sneks = one 0.5-gram dose)

Prep time

5 minutes

Cook time

10–15 minutes

Note:

If you want to use this recipe for microdosing, use 2.4 grams of dried ground shrooms or 4.8 milliliters of Ethanol Extraction. This will give you 1 microdose per snek.

Method

1 Place the pomegranate juice, sweetener and lemon juice in a medium saucepan and gently heat until warm. Do not bring to a boil.

2 Add in the agar-agar or gelatin super-slowly and whisk until combined.

3 Remove from the heat and stir in the Ethanol Extraction or the powdered shrooms. Note, if using extract: Alcohol is flammable, so make sure the pan is near NO open flames at this point.

4 Carefully pour or spoon the mixture into your gummy snek molds, or if you have a cooking syringe, use that. It's a lot easier.

5 Refrigerate for 4 hours.

6 Before eating, mix the sugar and citric acid together in a bowl, then roll the sneks in the mixture. Because of the acid and the nature of these (being made from juice), the sugar and acid will draw the liquid out of the sneks and make them wet, so sour them up and then eat them immediately.

7 For any that you don't want to consume immediately, store them pre-acid in an airtight container in the fridge, away from children. Consume within 2 weeks and sour them up before eating.

Shroom Shatter

Ingredients

4 cups white sugar

1½ cups light corn syrup

1 cup water

1 tablespoon flavor extract of your choice

7 grams dried shrooms, ground to a powder OR 14 milliliters Ethanol Extraction (page 28)

Servings

14 (depending on your molds). One 0.5-gram dose is two candies in our recipe.

Prep time

5 minutes

Cook time

25 minutes

Method

1 Combine the sugar, corn syrup and water in a medium saucepan over a medium-high heat.

2 Stir until the sugar is totally dissolved and bring to a boil, then stop stirring.

3 Place your candy thermometer (or point your laser) in the pan and when it reaches 300°F/150°C, pull the pan off the heat straightaway.

4 Wait until the temperature cools to 250°F/120°C, then add in the extract and the shrooms or Ethanol Extraction. Stir to combine. Note: Alcohol is flammable, so make sure the pan is near NO open flames at this point.

5 Pour into your candy molds and cool at room temperature for an hour.

6 Store in an airtight container away from children for up to a month.

Raspberry Magic Carpets

Ingredients

3 cups ripe or frozen raspberries (add ½ cup water if frozen)

3 tablespoons honey

3 teaspoons fresh lemon juice

4 grams ground mushrooms

Servings

8 (one roll-up = one 0.5-gram dose)

Prep time

15 minutes

Cook time

6–8 hours

Method

1 Preheat oven to lowest temperature (ideally around 140°F/60°C).

2 Puree the berries, honey and lemon juice (plus water if needed) in a food processor until smooth.

3 Stir in the ground shrooms evenly.

4 Pour onto a baking sheet lined with high-quality plastic wrap (the cheap stuff will melt), or ideally a silicone baking mat (don't use foil, parchment, or waxed paper), and spread to ⅛ inch thick.

5 Place in oven and bake on your low heat for 6–8 hours (or use a food dehydrator if you have one), until completely dried.

6 Cut into 8 long pieces.

7 Roll the roll-ups, store in airtight container away from children and consume within 2 weeks.

Sour Berry Magic Carpets

Ingredients

3 cups ripe or frozen blackberries and blueberries (add ½ cup water if frozen)

3 tablespoons honey

3 teaspoons fresh lemon juice

4 grams ground mushrooms

¼ cup caster sugar

1½ teaspoons citric acid

Servings

8

Prep time

15 minutes

Cook time

6–8 hours

Method

1 Preheat oven to lowest temperature (ideally around 140°F/60°C).

2 Puree the berries, honey and lemon juice (plus water if needed) in a food processor until smooth.

3 Stir in the ground shrooms evenly.

4 Pour onto a baking sheet lined with high-quality plastic wrap (the cheap stuff will melt), or ideally a silicone baking mat (don't use foil, parchment, or waxed paper), and spread to ⅛ inch thick.

5 Place in oven and bake on your low heat for 6–8 hours (or use a food dehydrator if you have one), until completely dried.

6 Cut into 8 long pieces.

7 Mix the citric acid and sugar together in a bowl, then drag each piece through the mixture, making sure it sticks to both sides.

8 Roll the roll-ups, store in airtight container away from children and consume within 2 weeks.

A Word about Microdosing

As you might recall if you've read our first book, you know that we are both fairly experienced fans of microdosing, the practice of taking "subtherapeutic" amounts of psilocybin mushrooms (or, for some people, other psychoactives) in order not to get high but instead as a precursor to going about our daily work and leisure lives feeling more creative, happier, more able to deal with daily stresses and generally more well balanced.

While microdosing has likely been going on for as long as psychedelics have been around (Terence McKenna posited the theory that psilocybin mushrooms may have helped early humans by heightening their senses and stamina, enabling them to hunt more effectively), it has been popularized in recent years by Dr. James Fadiman, a psychologist and writer who has long been active in the field of psychedelic research, and was in fact a lecturer in psychedelic studies (dream job, but we're not jealous, it's fine). At a psychedelic research conference in 2011, he discussed survey data he had collected from microdosing experimenters—including data about the use of microdoses as an alternative to drugs like Adderall and as a way to alleviate conditions like depression and chronic fatigue syndrome. The survey respondents told him that they were better creative thinkers when microdosing, more open to new ideas and increasingly able to search for innovative solutions. Dr. Fadiman was subsequently invited onto the podcast of tech-bro extraordinaire Tim Ferris, whose listenership is interested in anything to do with "biohacking" or increasing their productivity or ability to problem-solve at work. They self-experimented and many found that microdosing worked, so the practice spread across Silicon Valley swiftly, and the media became interested. Thanks to the subsequent reportage, many more people have been inspired to try this method and see if it works for them. In fact, since our last book microdosing seems not only more prevalent but also more accepted by mainstream voices, perhaps due to an increased amount of research in this area (but also maybe because it works?). We'll discuss some of the research a little later, but recent popular writing on microdosing can also be found in novelist Ayelet Waldman's book *A Really Good Day: How Microdosing Made a Mega Difference in my Mood, My Marriage, and My Life,* in which she writes about using small-dose psychedelics over a thirty-day period to help deal with her mood and anxiety disorders as well as traumatic life experiences.

The point of microdosing, as mentioned above, is *not* to get high. The goal is to take an almost imperceptible amount of your chosen psychedelic in order to stimulate creativity, focus, stamina and a general sense of well-being without any of the swirly reality visuals and the intense hallucinations of higher dose psychedelic trips. With a microdose, you tap into all the most useful and usable effects of psilocybin while avoiding those that remove you from the world of functioning humans.

The research

So what does the research have to say on this exciting new method of potential self-improvement? At the time of writing, not a great deal! A handful of studies have so far been conducted, and although they claim microdosing improves a variety of attributes including mood, energy, creative thought (as well as decreasing negative emotions), they tend to rely on self-reporting and participants knowing that they are microdosing. Why are these measures a problem? Well, if you know you've been microdosing, you will probably be hoping that it will do something positive, and when asked about it, your hope for a beneficial effect may mean that you tend to overemphasize what you're actually feeling. Indeed at least one recent study has found that a participant's expectation from microdosing has a strong effect on what they self-report on when asked about short-term psychological change (creativity, mindfulness and general well-being). When you strip away this expectation, by exploring participants' ratings over long periods of time when expectation may drop away, these anticipated improvements don't appear to manifest themselves. That's not to say that there are no benefits to microdosing; they just may not be the ones we *expect*. The study described previously found that longer-term effects include reductions in mind wandering, anxiety and depression, but also increased engagement with art and nature. One potentially negative trait that was slightly increased in long-term microdosing studies was *neuroticism*, a term which is argued over to this day in psychology, but is generally thought to relate to your ability to handle stress. If your "neuroticism," so defined, is increased due to microdosing, you may find it more difficult to handle the regular day-to-day stresses of life. Such early findings show that although microdosing appears to have small positive effects, it may not be for everyone (especially if you're already susceptible to stress).

Taking a step back from the research for a second and looking at the question more generally, the effect of microdosing is incredibly hard to measure. For one, you're looking to understand how small, sub-perceptual doses may bring about very small changes. As the old adage goes in science, "small effect; large sample," meaning that you need lots of people to participate in your study to get a good understanding of what's going on. The next issue is that tricky-to-define concepts like creativity and mindfulness are hard to measure scientifically, so just as binoculars wouldn't help you smell a flower, you need to make sure that you're not using the wrong measurement method when it comes to psychological concepts like these. Finally, as mentioned before, we have the expectation effect and the problem with self-reported data. As far as problems go this is probably the easiest to overcome. Clinical drug trials deal with this problem all the time using placebo-controlled studies, where half your participants unwittingly get a sugar pill and half get the dose. You then compare your findings between the groups and see if your active dose does better than your pill full of lies, and if it does you potentially have a viable treatment. From some of the studies currently in process, the placebo effect is being incorporated to help address this issue. As we've said at the start of this book, if you're interested we'd encourage you to find a study and participate...for science!

As we wrote in our previous book, from our own experience and that reported by many others, microdosing is sort of like being on a mood enhancer or an antidepressant but without any of the terrible side effects, which is exactly how many people are using microdoses. Many people have reported that microdosing helped them deal with depression, OCD, ADD and eating and anxiety disorders, making this a potentially viable alternative to the selective serotonin re-uptake inhibitors (SSRIs) that are routinely prescribed for such conditions, and which come with the risk of suicidal thoughts, sexual dysfunction, restlessness, inter-cranial bleeding and perhaps the worst of all, pleasureless orgasm.

However, we shouldn't give the impression that there are no downsides to microdosing. Increased empathy means that you can be more emotional (top tip: don't watch *Dumbo*) and while it's easier to focus for long periods, it's also easy to become distracted, and stay distracted, if you allow your mind to wander off topic. In our experience, using psilocybin is preferable to LSD as the high is somewhat milder and isn't too inward-looking, which can be fine but can really get in the way of you going about your daily routine. We also find that there's more of a body-experience with psilocybin, and we also find it easier to accurately dose with shrooms that we've grown ourselves than with LSD for which we're relying on someone else (but it should also be noted that we just prefer shrooms to LSD any day of the week, so part of that is just our bias). Of course, there's also a suggestion that the sense of well-being we feel from microdosing is just a placebo effect—and perhaps a portion of that is true. But there's a reason doctors prescribe placebos sometimes; whether the medicine has an effect or not, the outcome is the same.

How to microdose

Like all dosing when it comes to mind-altering substances, what's right for someone else might not be what's right for you. It's generally accepted that a microdose is one tenth of a "therapeutic" dose; that is, a dose that you would usually use to get the full effects. You'll read that other people take anywhere between 0.1 and 0.5 grams of dried shrooms, but as already discussed in this book, the effect that shrooms have on you can be affected by the strain of shrooms, the extraction method, how much you've eaten, how much you've drunk in the last twenty-four hours and so on and so on. What you're planning to do while microdosed may also affect your dosing choice; if you're sitting at home or in a cafe and writing a novel you might chance a higher dose, while if you've got to go into an office or work environment and be a highly capable human being who's accountable to others, you may want to err on the side of caution. It's all going to be trial and error!

As ever, we suggest dosing low at first. We had effects from as little as 0.1 gram of dried shrooms, but a lot of people consider a microdose to be .35 gram, given that 3.5 grams is a generally accepted "normal" dose (though high in our opinion, especially for newcomers!). While some people even advocate going as high as 0.5 grams, we personally feel that this is on the edge of an active dose (and also why it's the dose we chose for the recipes in this book). You've got nothing to lose by starting low, but as anyone who's dosed slightly too high will tell you, missing the sweet spot with microdosing isn't that fun. It's not awful, and it's certainly not so bad that you can't cope, but if you take too much you will be stuck in this weird nether zone where you're not high, exactly, but you're not straight enough to do much of anything at all, certainly not do your work or carry out the tasks you wanted to, which is frustrating and you'll want the feeling to pass faster, which it won't. Starting low means that you can try a slightly higher dose until you find it gives the effects you're looking for, and you can stick there until it's necessary to change.

The question that arises quickly when you've tried microdosing once and found that you like it is this: how often could, or should, you do it? As always, we recommend caution when it comes to bringing something into your life that you might become overly reliant on. We all get excited and slightly too passionate when we find something new that works and feels like it's making us fulfill our potential. Of course we do; it's an addictive feeling. But we also should consider that anytime we depart from normality a little, we have to give ourselves adequate time to come back and reset before we depart again. Dr. Fadiman's suggested microdosing schedule, for the best effects, looks like this:

Day One: Microdose.
Day Two: Observe any residual effects.
Day Three: Take a break.
Day Four: Repeat.

While it's only anecdotal, our own experience with microdosing supports the above. When we first got into it we were dosing more regularly, (on days one and three), and we found that this did not adequately allow for us to come back to a settled starting point before we micro-dosed again. As ever with any sort of substance (including coffee and cigarettes), if something becomes too much of a regular habit it can be too easy to convince yourself that you *need* it in order to, say, tackle a difficult problem at work or maybe write a really great song or whatever you want to do that's important to you. A one-day-on/two-days-off cycle prevents this to a significant degree, although of course there is always potential for psychological dependency to creep in. If you're interested in bringing microdosing into your routine, it's good to have clearly de-fined expectations or goals. If you're simply using this method as a rea-son to take mushrooms on a daily basis, or to escape the sharp edges of a reality that you're not entirely happy with, then you should be striv-ing towards a change in that reality rather than finding an excuse to get away from it. We don't condone regular use of psychedelics (or any-thing) as a way to avoid real life.

You'll also have to consider that one day you'll have to stop. Let's say that you find that microdosing works perfectly for you; it stimulates you to work better and with longer periods of creativity and concentra-tion. You start doing it maybe a couple of times a week and your work life is greatly enhanced. One issue here is that you can become reliant on the microdose. If you start to feel that you work best while dosing, it's incredibly difficult to convince yourself that you're still good without it. Perhaps you're in an environment where you can microdose till the day you die. That's great; most of us aren't. Not to be Professor Buzz Killington about this, but remember that one day you'll likely have to stop microdosing and you need to be able to be a happy, productive, functioning member of society with no assistance at all. This isn't to say that you shouldn't microdose; this is just to say that you will always need to come back to Earth.

Our method

When we microdose we work to a dose of 0.1 gram, given that our shrooms generally produce effects at 1 gram per person. There are a number of ways that we've been microdosing since our last book came out, although our favorite method is still the one using the Ethanol Extraction detailed on page 28. This extraction contained 10 grams of active material in 20 milliliters of alcohol, meaning that 1 milliliter contained one 0.5-gram mushroom dose.

To create microdoses, we took 2 milliliters of the Basic Ethanol Extraction and added this to 100 milliliters of orange juice. We then split this into 10 milliliter portions and put each 10 milliliter portion into one compartment of an ice cube tray, then popped the ice cube tray into the freezer. This created ten separate microdoses of 0.1 gram per ice cube. We then popped each dose out and melted it into a larger glass of juice or simply waited for it to melt in a glass and took it like a shot.

You can use any liquid of your choice for this; juice was a good choice for us as it tastes good and is relatively healthy. You can even just use water, though we'd recommend something with a strong taste to counteract the taste of the extraction itself.

One concern with this method is the breakdown of the active ingredient at room temperature. This is why we recommend freezing the psilocybin-containing OJ into dosed cubes.

Most people advocate microdosing in the morning, but this is largely because most people want to feel the effects throughout the workday, and because you've just had an eight-hour fast, and so will be dosing on a relatively empty stomach. Realistically you can microdose at any time of day, though you should avoid taking your dose too close to bedtime just in case you struggle getting to sleep.

Please remember while experimenting with microdosing that you, as an adult human, are not only responsible for yourself but for other people, and that your actions in the world have consequences not only for you but for others as well. For this reason, don't do anything while microdosing that you wouldn't do after a couple of beers, and dose safely. We all wanna be good guys, so keep that in mind.

About the Authors

Virginia Haze is a nomadic writer and editor with a long history of both writing about and using intoxicants in all their forms, though not always at the same time. She's written for drug culture magazines, worked on many step-by-step cultivation guides and learned to grow mushrooms under the expert tutelage of Dr. Mandrake. After beginning her growing career for personal use, she spent years perfecting her techniques and studying the science of psilocybin cultivation to allow her to grow on a commercial scale. Her specific mycological interests involve psilocybin extractions and modifying traditional grow methods. As well as sitting in her grow rooms to watch her little fungi make their way into the world, Virginia enjoys puns, '80s B-movies and fermenting any damn thing she can get her hands on.

Dr. K. Mandrake is a lover of hallucinogens from both a scientific and a recreational perspective. His long and varied education has mostly centered on biology, toxicology and mycology, culminating in a PhD in microbiology, which greatly influenced his home growing methods. He cultivates all types of mushrooms (psychedelic and purely delicious) from his base in the U.K., and outside of his more traditional academic position, he teaches others how to grow their own mushrooms in a sustainable, healthy and affordable way. Some say they're married to the job; Dr. Mandrake says he's married to the mushrooms. His specific mycological interests include agar work and bulk substrate methods. He enjoys turning his kitchen into a makeshift laboratory, climbing to the top of very high mountains and kicking back with a home-brewed beer to play indie video games.

Learn the Art and Science of Growing High Quality Magic Mushrooms

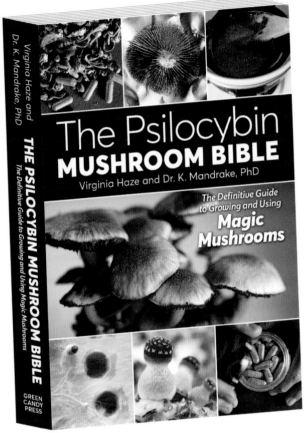

The Psilocybin Mushroom Bible explains how to set up a safe, discreet and effective mushroom grow operation that will provide you with an endless supply of shrooms in a short amount of time.

Growing perfect psilocybin mushrooms has never been easier.

A WHOLE NEW FLAVOR!